Ray Collins

440 More Snappy Sermon Starters

by

PAUL E. HOLDCRAFT

ABINGDON PRESS
New York • Nashville

440 MORE SNAPPY SERMON STARTERS

SET UP, PRINTED, AND BOUND BY THE PARTHENON PRESS, AT NASHVILLE, TENNESSEE, UNITED STATES OF AMERICA

PREFACE

If you have a dollar, and I have a dollar, and we swap dollars, each of us will have but a dollar. If you have an idea, and I have an idea, and we swap ideas, each of us will have two ideas.

Here are many ideas, interpretations, and techniques offered for the use or inspiration of one who is seeking to unfold the eternal truths of the Holy Bible and the Christian faith. In this collection of sermon starters are the accumulated wisdom and methods of many devout and capable preachers and teachers, of the past and the present, of many denominations, and from a great variety of sources. Many of the starters are sermon outlines, which may either be used completely or serve as a stimulus for the development of one's own outlines. No starter is presumed to be complete or comprehensive. There is nothing *to read* in this volume, but plenty *to study,* along with your Bible and concordance. Only as the user adds to, takes from, revises, rethinks, and uses these starters as a mental stimulant will he realize their full value. One's own concepts, the methods learned in seminary or through one's own experimentation, and many other factors should help to determine the sermon that develops from any of these starters.

The collection is planned for use throughout the Christian year and in any situation. Some starters are from sermons on special days; others are thoroughly general. The key words given in the Index will enable a minister to find a starter to fit the theme of the sermon he is planning. The arrangement of starters in the first two sections according to the order of their biblical texts will also save him much time and searching.

Gratefully I acknowledge my indebtedness to many who have given permissions, and to many others whose outlines I have felt privileged to use because they were evidently in the public domain. Wherever I have known of my indebtedness, I have given proper credit.

PAUL E. HOLDCRAFT

CONTENTS

I
Old Testament Texts

1. THREE EXPERIMENTS, THREE FAILURES

"When they were in the field, . . . Cain rose up against Abel his brother, and slew him." *Gen. 4:8*

I. The Family Idea Won't Keep Men Right.
(Cain and Abel were brothers.)

II. Religious Ceremonial Won't Keep Men Right.
(Cain and Abel both offered sacrifices.)

III. Religious Persecution Won't Keep Men Right.
(Cain killed his brother, but a voice cried against him.)

IV. What Will Keep Men Right?
(The love of God through Jesus Christ)

—Joseph Parker

2. THE RAINBOW IN THE CLOUD

"I do set my bow in the cloud, and it shall be for a token of a covenant between me and the earth." *Gen. 9:13*

The rainbow

1. Is a pledge of God's fidelity to his word.
2. Is an emblem of the covenant of redemption.
3. Is an apt emblem of union and harmony in the midst of diversity.
4. Well represents man's present state of probation and discipline.
5. Is a striking emblem of human hopes.
6. Affords us a glimpse of the magnificence of the heavenly world, and the glory of God.

—Roswell D. Hitchcock

3. WHEN RELIGION IS SIDETRACKED

"And Terah died in Haran." *Gen. 11:32*

Terah, the father of Abraham, started for the promised land but tarried in Haran, about halfway, and died there.

I. What Caused Him to Sidetrack the Will of God?
1. Temporal prosperity? Haran was probably a good place for his cattle to graze.
2. Ease and pleasure?
3. Indecision? Just couldn't make up his mind?

II. Whatever the Cause, It Was a Costly Thing.
1. He never arrived in Palestine.
2. He died in a pagan land.

Application: Many today are allowing the temporal things of the world to have preference over the will of God. Many who have started out for the Promised Land die short of the goal.

4. OUT OF THE OLD, INTO THE NEW

"The Lord had said unto Abram, Get thee out of thy country, and from thy kindred, and from thy father's house, unto a land that I will shew thee." *Gen. 12:1*

The call of Abram was twofold, "out of" and "into." This is suggestive of the call every child of God receives.

I. As Christians, We Are "Called Out."
1. Out of the old life of sin; slavery to Satan
2. "Come out from among them"—evil companions.
3. "Who is on the Lord's side?"
4. Some are called upon to leave homes, dear ones, good positions, in order to serve the Lord in a special manner—missionaries, ministers, etc.

II. As Christians, We Are "Called Into."
1. Into a life of fellowship with and service for Christ

2. Often it means into a new circle of friends.
3. Into the Promised Land (Text)

5. THE PRESENCE OF GOD

"Thou God seest me."

Gen. 16:13

A poor Egyptian slave girl, Hagar, spoke these words. Her life had become unendurable, and so she ran away into the wilderness, and an angel of God came to her and told her to return. Hagar's words teach us:

I. There Is a Lesson of God's Watchful Providence.
1. When we are exposed to great temptations
2. In any time of trouble or sorrow
3. In time of prayer
4. When we have to make difficult decisions

II. God's Presence Ought to Be the Great Joy of Our Life.
1. Here
2. Hereafter

—A. G. Mortimer

6. THE OFFERING OF ISAAC

"Take now thy son, thine only son Isaac, whom thou lovest, and get thee into the land of Moriah; and offer him there for a burnt offering upon one of the mountains which I will tell thee of."

Gen. 22:2

Certain features of this severe trial resemble some of the operations of divine providence known to us:

1. Often we are exposed to great trials without any reason being assigned for their infliction.

2. Even in our severest trials we have hope in the delivering mercy of God.

3. Obedience on our part has ever been followed by special tokens of God's approval.

4. The supreme lesson is that we should completely subjugate our wills to God's. (Jesus in Gethsemane.)

—Joseph Parker

7. SELECTING A LIFE COMPANION

"They called Rebekah, and said unto her, Wilt thou go with this man? And she said, I will go."

Gen. 24:58

1. Young people do well to accept the wise and loving counsel of parents in the matter of choosing life companions.

2. Your chances for happiness are best if you select a mate from among the people of God. ("Be ye not unequally yoked.")

3. Prayer and faith in God are essential to happy and successful mating.

4. Rebekah's qualities: domesticated; kindly disposition; a devoted daughter; she felt God was arranging her union with Isaac.

5. True love marked this ancient courtship and marriage.

—Dinsdale T. Young

8. LIFE ON GOD'S PLAN

"He [Isaac] builded an altar there, and called upon the name of the Lord, and pitched his tent there: and there Isaac's servants digged a well." *Gen. 26:25*

I. "[Isaac] Builded an Altar."
1. Worship was his first concern in his new location.
2. Worship was a first concern of the pilgrims and adventurers in early American history.

II. "And [Isaac] Pitched His Tent There."
1. Established his home, but not until he had first "called upon the name of the Lord."

III. "THERE ISAAC'S SERVANTS DIGGED A WELL."
1. Necessity for their own well-being
2. A service rendered the entire community

—From *Life on God's Plan* by H. R. Mackintosh

9. RELIGION IN ADVERSITY

"Joseph's master took him, and put him into the prison."

Gen. 39:20

I. HE WAS A GOOD MAN IN A BAD PLACE.
1. Not guilty of any wrongdoing
2. Many good men have been imprisoned, though innocent: Jeremiah, Daniel, John the Baptist, Paul, Silas, Peter, John, etc.
3. The plots of the wicked seem to succeed for a season.

II. JOSEPH RETAINS HIS FAITH IN GOD AND MAINTAINS HIS RELIGIOUS INTEGRITY.
1. "Stone walls do not a prison make."
2. Joseph didn't become morose and churlish.
3. Maintained cheerful disposition
4. Friendly and faithful to fellow prisoners
5. Useful to his jailer

III. ALL THINGS WORKED TOGETHER FOR GOOD.
1. God's presence and blessing with him
2. The chain of providential events
3. Deliverance
4. Leadership

10. ALL'S WELL THAT ENDS WELL

"Pharaoh said unto Joseph, See, I have set thee over all the land of Egypt." *Gen. 41:41*

I. JOSEPH'S TROUBLES
1. Hated by his brothers; maltreated; life threatened
2. Sold into Egypt; slavery
3. Accused of crime he didn't commit; imprisoned

II. JOSEPH'S DEPORTMENT
1. Did not become bitter
2. Used his wisdom to help others
3. His conduct and ability attracted attention of the authorities.

III. JOSEPH'S EXALTATION
1. Made prime minister
2. Opportunity to serve his fellow men
3. Humiliation often leads to exaltation.
4. "All's well that ends well."

11. SINS AGAINST CHILDREN

"Do not sin against the child."

Gen. 42:22

We sin against children:

I. WHEN WE FAIL TO GIVE THEM THE BEST POSSIBLE PARENTS
1. A child's inherent right to be wellborn

II. WHEN WE ARE INDIFFERENT TO THEIR EDUCATION
1. Secular education
2. Religious education

III. WHEN WE FAIL TO PROVIDE A WHOLESOME ENVIRONMENT FOR THEM

12. LIFT UP YOUR EYES, AND LOOK!

"And it came to pass in those days, when Moses was grown, that he went out unto his brethren, and looked on their burdens."

Exod. 2:11

I. SOME PREFER NOT TO SEE THE BURDENS OF OTHERS.
1. They pretend not to see. "None so blind as. . . ."
2. Lacking in sympathy
3. Fear their time, energy, and purse may become involved.

4. Illustration: The Priest and the Levite went by "on the other side" of the road.

II. WHAT THEY MISS WHO FAIL TO LOOK AND HELP
1. The thrill of relieving distress
2. The satisfaction of duty done
3. The commendation of the Lord. "Well done. . . ."
4. The reward: "Enter thou into the joy of thy Lord."

Application:
"Lift up your eyes, and look on the fields."
The near view; the far view

13. UNOBSERVED SINS

"He looked this way and that way, and when he saw that there was no man, he slew the Egyptian." *Exod. 2:12*

I. TO THINK ONESELF UNOBSERVED OFTEN MAKES WAY FOR SIN.
1. Similar scene in the New Testament—Peter warming by the enemy's fire
2. Often those who are highly honored and respected at home act quite differently when far away from home.
3. Often in the seclusion of the home people act very differently than in public.

II. UNOBSERVED SINS USUALLY BECOME OBSERVED.
1. Moses' act was observed.
2. "Be sure your sin will find you out."
3. If no one else sees, remember the eye of God observes both good and evil.

14. THE BURNING BUSH—AN EMBLEM OF THE CHURCH

"The angel of the Lord appeared unto him in a flame of fire out of the midst of a bush: and he looked, and, behold, the bush burned with fire, and the bush was not consumed." *Exod. 3:2*

I. THE TRUE CHURCH OF GOD IS NOT ASSOCIATED WITH EARTHLY GRANDEUR AND MAGNIFICENCE.

II. THE CONDITION OF THE CHURCH HAS EVER BEEN THAT OF TRIAL AND SUFFERING.

III. THE CHURCH HAS WITHIN IT THE ELEMENT OF PERPETUITY. ("The gates of hell shall not prevail against it.")

15. TAKE TIME TO BE HOLY

"Moses said, I will now turn aside, and see this great sight, why the bush is not burnt." *Exod. 3:3*

1. Like Moses, we must turn aside from routine if we are to see and profit by the manifestations of God.

2. Humble environment is not a bar to the presence of God.

3. The Deity is to be approached with becoming reverence.

4. The Church may suffer in the fires of persecution, but it is not consumed.

16. GOD GIVE US MEN

"Provide out of all the people able men, such as fear God, men of truth, hating covetousness; and place such over them." *Exod. 18:21*

Thousands of years have passed since these words were spoken, but they still summarize the essential qualities that leaders in both church and state should have.

I. "ABLE MEN"
1. Ability; efficiency; intelligence
2. Many little men in big places they can't fill

II. "SUCH AS FEAR GOD"
1. Men of prayer
2. Church attenders

3. Bible readers
4. In touch with God

III. "Men of Truth"
1. Truthfulness; honesty; sincerity
2. "The truth shall make . . . free."
3. "Truth is mighty and it will prevail."
4. "Truth, crushed to earth, shall rise again."

IV. "Hating Covetousness"
1. Not merely personally free from it, but having a positive attitude of hate for it
2. Too many covetous men in public office
3. Covetousness brings on graft, corruption, dishonesty.

17. WHY KEEP THE SABBATH

"Remember the sabbath day, to keep it holy." *Exod. 20:8*

Reasons for observing the Sabbath:

1. God commands it.
2. God claims it as his own day.
3. It is a memorial of a completed creation, and of Christ's resurrection.
4. Our forefathers have profited by keeping it.
5. It is a blessed emblem and foretaste of heaven.

Application: "It is a poor preparation for your first Sabbath in eternity to have misspent your last Sabbath on earth."

18. SPIRITUAL BEAUTY

"Moses wist not that the skin of his face shone while he talked with him." *Exod. 34:29*

Spiritual beauty is loveliest when it is unconsciously possessed.

I. The Face of Moses Was Transfigured by the Glory of the Eternal.
1. It happened as he talked with God and was oblivious of what was happening to himself.
2. Prayer transfigures: Jesus on the mount.

II. Some Seek This Spiritual Beauty Improperly.
1. Affected humility
2. Charity to be seen of men. "The sound of a trumpet"
3. Remember: "Satan's heart was lifted up because of his beauty."

Application: "If a man once gets a good look at Jesus Christ, he will never be the same again."

19. CHARACTER ASSASSINATION

"Thou shalt not go up and down as a talebearer among thy people." *Lev. 19:16*

1. Character is in the keeping, and therefore at the mercy, of acquaintances.
2. Character may be ruthlessly shattered by sinister whisperings.
3. Character is so precious that its traducers should be loathed.

—W. H. Jellie

20. THE CHRISTIAN PILGRIM

"We are journeying unto the place of which the Lord said, I will give it you: come thou with us, and we will do thee good." *Num. 10:29*

I. "We Are Journeying."
1. "I am a stranger, . . . and a sojourner, as all my fathers were." Ps. 39:12.
2. All are traveling upon the level of time.
3. Each day finds us in a new location. "Ye have not passed this way heretofore." Josh. 3:4.

II. As Christians, We Are Going Somewhere.
1. Not going around in circles
2. Our destination: "the place

of which the Lord said, I will give it you." Promised land

3. "A city which hath foundations, whose builder and maker is God."

III. "COME THOU WITH US."

1. Christians want to share the road.
2. Plenty of room for all on the King's Highway

IV. "WE WILL DO THEE GOOD."

1. The Church a "mutual-aid Society"
2. "We share each other's woes,
   Each other's burdens bear."
3. The Church exists for one purpose—to do good.

21. THE SPIRIT OF CALEB

"But my servant Caleb, because he had another spirit with him, and hath followed me fully, him will I bring into the land."

Num. 14:24

I. GOD'S TESTIMONY CONCERNING CALEB (He had "another spirit with him.")

1. Optimistic, trustful: "Let us go up at once."
2. Conciliatory
3. Cheerful
4. Prompt
5. Followed the Lord fully

II. THE REWARD PROMISED ("Him will I bring into the land.")

1. The promise was fulfilled at last.
2. "All's well that ends well."

—From *Seeds and Saplings*

22. HERE LONG ENOUGH

"The Lord our God spake unto us in Horeb, saying, Ye have dwelt long enough in this mount."

Deut. 1:6

What God said to Moses and his followers, he has been saying at intervals to many individuals as well as groups, down through the ages.

I. TO SOME WHO LIVE IN THE REALM OF PLEASURE HE SAYS, "YE HAVE DWELT HERE LONG ENOUGH."

II. THE WORDS ARE SOMETIMES SPOKEN TO THOSE WHO LIVE IN EASE AND PROSPERITY.

III. GOD IS COMPELLED TO SAY IT TO THOSE WHO ARE GUILTY OF WRONGDOING.

IV. HE MAY HAVE TO SAY IT TO CHRISTIAN WORKERS WHO HAVE STAYED TOO LONG IN ONE PLACE AND ARE NEEDED ELSEWHERE.

1. Ministers
2. Local church officers

V. IT IS EVEN POSSIBLE GOD SAYS IT TO THOSE ENGAGED IN WORSHIP.

1. Mount Horeb a place of worship and revelation
2. Peter wanted to stay on the Mount of Transfiguration, but Jesus thought of the needs in the valley.

VI. SOMEDAY THE WORDS WILL BE SPOKEN TO EACH OF US.

1. Now we are strangers and sojourners on the earth.
2. Someday we shall be called hence.

23. AN OUNCE OF PREVENTION

"When thou buildest a new house, then thou shalt make a battlement for thy roof, that thou bring not blood upon thine house, if any man fall from thence."

Deut. 22:8

The word "battlement" here refers to a wall, raised several feet higher than the house roof, to serve two purposes—fortification, and to prevent persons' accidentally falling off.

It seems that as long ago as the

time of Moses there was a religious awareness of responsibility for eliminating hazards to human life.

I. THE TEXT IS AN ANSWER TO CAIN'S QUESTION, "AM I MY BROTHER'S KEEPER?"
   1. Certain social responsibilities are inescapable.
   2. Especially true of factories; public places
   3. We need boards of health, fire inspectors, traffic regulations, building codes, etc.
   4. In a complex society such as ours there is no such thing as complete personal liberty.

II. THE TEXT IS ANOTHER WAY OF SAYING, "AN OUNCE OF PREVENTION IS WORTH A POUND OF CURE."
   1. Better a high wall on the house than to endanger a life (oriental roofs used for social purposes).
   2. Better to prohibit the liquor traffic than to care for the victims later.
   3. "Better build a fence on the cliff than a hospital below to care for those who fall off."
   4. This principle applies to war.
   5. It applies to all sins; all hazards.

III. THE TEXT SUGGESTS A MAIN FUNCTION OF THE CHURCH.
   1. Better to prevent sin than to deal with results of sin.
   2. Better to train up children in the way they should go than to seek to reclaim them later.

24. A CHANGELESS GOD IN A CHANGING WORLD

"The eternal God is thy refuge, and underneath are the everlasting arms." *Deut. 33:27*

The words are part of Moses' valedictory, spoken to reassure and comfort Israel. We have great need for this text in these chaotic times.

I. THIS IS A CHANGING WORLD
   1. "Change and decay in all around I see."
   2. Forms of government change.
   3. Maps of the world change overnight.
   4. Cities thought impregnable are destroyed in hours.
   5. Paupers become rich; rich become paupers.
   6. Humanity subject to change
   7. "The captains and the kings depart."

II. WE HAVE AN ETERNAL GOD.
   1. "I change not."
   2. "Jesus Christ the same yesterday, and to day, and for ever."
   3. ". . . Behind the dim unknown,
      Standeth God within the shadow,
      keeping watch above his own."
      —Lowell
   4. "Underneath are the everlasting arms."
   5. "I am with you alway."

25. LOVE'S LABOR IS NEVER LOST

"But thou shalt not go over thither." *Deut. 34:4*

Very few are allowed to live long enough to reach all their goals and complete all their labors.

I. IT IS TRUE OF THE THINKER.
   1. Edison: "We don't know one thousandth of one per cent of anything yet."
   2. To every thinker who struggles to reach metaphysical or scientific certitude there come the words of the text.

II. IT IS TRUE OF MEN OF ACTION.
1. Reformers; statesmen; philanthropists; scientists
2. Ministers and missionaries
3. Many of the greatest artists, composers, poets, and statesmen have died with the feeling they were failures.

III. IN THE ECONOMY OF GOD, "LOVE'S LABOR IS NEVER LOST."
1. Young shoulders and stout hearts carry on.
2. "Other men laboured, and ye are entered into their labours."
3. Moses failed to realize his ambitions on earth, but his place in history is forever secure.

26. SIN IS PROGRESSIVE

"When I saw among the spoils a goodly Babylonish garment, and two hundred shekels of silver, and a wedge of gold of fifty shekels weight, then I coveted them, and took them; and, behold, they are hid in the earth in the midst of my tent, and the silver under it."
Josh. 7:21

1. The head: "I saw."
2. The heart: "I coveted."
3. The hand: "I took."
4. The hurry: "I hid."
5. The horror: Achan was stoned. (v. 25.)

—T. K.

27. YOUR DAY OF DECISION

"Choose you this day whom ye will serve." *Josh. 24:15*

I. CHOOSE YOU THIS DAY WHOM YE WILL SERVE.
(The issue must be faced.)

II. CHOOSE YOU THIS DAY WHOM YE WILL SERVE.
(It is a personal choice.)

III. CHOOSE YOU THIS DAY WHOM YE WILL SERVE.
("Now is the accepted time; . . . now is the day of salvation." II Cor. 6:2.)

IV. CHOOSE YOU THIS DAY WHOM YE WILL SERVE.
(Christ or Satan. Can't be neutral.)

V. CHOOSE YOU THIS DAY WHOM YE WILL SERVE.
(Christianity is something *to do*, as well as *to be*.)

28. TAKE YOUR BATTLE STATION

"They stood every man in his place round about the camp."
Judg. 7:21

Implications of the story of Gideon:

I. THE RACE IS NOT ALWAYS TO THE SWIFT, NOR THE BATTLE TO THE STRONG.
1. Napoleon said, "That army wins that gets there first with the most." He met his "Waterloo."
2. No student of history would say, "God is on the side of the heaviest battalions."
3. Midianites and Amalekites were as "grasshoppers . . . and . . . as the sand by the sea side for multitude" but went down to defeat before Gideon's valiants.

II. THE NEED OF THE HOUR IS A SENSE OF DEPENDENCE UPON GOD.
1. Gideon's band knew their need of God.
2. Our country needs this sense of dependence upon God.
3. The Church needs it. "Not by might, nor by power, but by my Spirit, saith the Lord."
4. We need it, personally.

III. A PLACE AND A TASK FOR EVERY CHRISTIAN.
   1. "Every man [stood] in his place." Victory.
   2. "To every man his work." No proxies.

29. THE ROYAL FAMILY OF GOD

"Each one resembled the children of a king." *Judg. 8:18*

I. WE BEAR THE KING'S IMAGE.
II. WE HAVE PRINCELY TITLES.
III. WE HAVE ACCESS TO THE KING HIMSELF.
IV. WE WEAR ROYAL APPAREL.
V. WE POSSESS A PRINCELY SPIRIT.

30. A GOOD WORD FOR MOTHERS-IN-LAW

"Orpah kissed her mother in law; but Ruth clave unto her." *Ruth 1:14*

I. THE STORY OF NAOMI IS THE STORY OF A NOBLE MOTHER-IN-LAW. (Read book of Ruth.)
II. WE LIST A FEW OF HER NOBLE QUALITIES:
   1. She accepted her daughters-in-law as her very own children.
   2. She was unfeignedly affectionate and considerate of them.
   3. She didn't allow their religions to mar her relations with them.
   4. She put their happiness above her own.
   5. She gave them good counsel, based on her own mature judgment and experience.
   6. She lived her religion instead of arguing it.

31. THE CHILD SAMUEL

"She bare a son, and called his name Samuel, saying, Because I have asked him of the Lord." *I Sam. 1:20*

He was:

1. A progressive child. "Samuel grew before the Lord," "grew on," "Samuel grew" (I Sam. 2:21, 26; 3:19).

2. A privileged child. "The Lord was with him" (I Sam. 3:19).

3. A powerful child. "None of his words [fell] to the ground" (I Sam. 3:19).

4. A prosperous child. "All Israel . . . knew [he] was established to be a prophet" (I Sam. 3:2).

—James Sprunt

32. HONORING GOD

"Them that honour me I will honour." *I Sam. 2:30*

I. HOW GOD MAY BE HONORED
   1. By acknowledging his government
   2. By trusting his word
   3. By obedience to his wishes
   4. By ascriptions of praise
   5. By reverence for his day, his Book, his house
   6. By humble service to others in his name
II. HOW GOD WILL HONOR US
   1. Adoption into his family.
   2. Help and comfort in tribulation
   3. Victory in death
   4. Immortality

33. THE BOY PROPHET

"The child Samuel ministered unto the Lord." *I Sam. 3:1*

Samuel was:

1. Asked of God *in prayer.* (I Sam. 1:20.)

2. Dedicated to God *in faith.* (I Sam. 1:28.)

3. Called by God *in grace.* (I Sam. 3:10.)

4. Approved by God *in service.* (I Sam. 3:19.)

34. "LORD, SPEAK TO ME!"

"Speak, Lord; for thy servant heareth." *I Sam. 3:9*

I. Through the Ages, by Many Voices, God Has Spoken to His Children.
   1. Audibly. Moses in the desert; on Sinai. Saul en route to Damascus. John on Patmos.
   2. Visions and dreams. Jacob; Ezekiel; Peter on the housetop.
   3. Through the prophets
   4. Through his Word; his Church. Isaiah's call.
   5. Acts of providence
   6. In nature. "He speaks to me everywhere."

II. To Hear God's Voice We Must:
   1. "Turn aside" as Moses did in the desert.
   2. "Be still" long enough to hear.
   3. Tune out static of the world. Elijah—storm, quake, fire, then the "still small voice."
   4. Be "in the Spirit on the Lord's day." If John had not been observing the day, we would not have the book of Revelation.
   5. Samuel's experience.

III. Answer "Yes" When He Calls.

35. MEN WITH GOD-TOUCHED HEARTS

"There went with him a band of men, whose hearts God had touched." *I Sam. 10:26*

What kind of men are men with God-touched hearts?

I. Spirit-Led Men
   1. Like Abraham: "He went out, not knowing whither."
   2. Philip the Evangelist
   3. Paul and Barnabas
   4. John on Patmos

II. Song-Filled Men
   1. David: "He hath put a new song in my mouth."
   2. Paul and Silas: songs in prison at midnight

III. Courageous Men
   1. Daniel
   2. The Hebrew worthies Shadrach, Meshach, Abednego,
   3. "The Lord is my helper, and I will not fear what man shall do unto me." (Heb. 13:6.)

IV. Witnesses for Christ
   1. The disciples "went every where preaching the word."
   2. Jesus: "Ye are witnesses."

36. A HILLBILLY MAKES GOOD

"And he sent, and brought him in. Now he was ruddy, and withal of a beautiful countenance, and goodly to look to. And the Lord said, Arise, anoint him: for this is he." *I Sam. 16:12.*

Some characteristics and accomplishments of the many-sided David:

I. Shepherd
   1. Knew all about sheep.
   2. Had a shepherd's heart.

II. Musician
   1. Made his own instruments and taught himself to play them.
   2. Headings of certain psalms indicate he was familiar with at least ten different musical instruments.

III. Poet and Hymn Writer
   1. The Psalter

IV. Athlete and Patriot
   1. Encounter with Goliath
   2. Man of war

V. King
   1. Probably Israel's best
   2. Ancestor of the King of kings

VI. Friend
   1. Revealed in his relations with Jonathan
   2. Read Ps. 133.

VII. Deeply Religious
   1. Loved God, God's house,

God's day, God's Word, and God's people.
2. Man of prayer

VIII. Could Shed Penitential Tears
1. Other monarchs of that time would not have given a second thought to sins.
2. Read Ps. 51.

IX. Looked into the Future
1. Planned that a great temple be erected in Jerusalem.
2. Solomon worked out the plans.

37. THE CHARACTER OF DAVID

"Behold, I have seen a son of Jesse the Bethlehemite, that is cunning in playing, and a mighty valiant man, and a man of war, and prudent in matters, and a comely person, and the Lord is with him."
I Sam. 16:18

Five distinct things are told us about David:

I. He Had a Worth-While Pastime.
1. "Cunning in playing"
2. Made his own musical instruments; played them; composed both words and music.
3. The Psalter.

II. He Was Patriotic.
1. "A . . . valiant man, . . . a man of war"

III. He Had Good Sense.
1. "Prudent in matters"

IV. He Was Good-Looking.
1. "A comely person"

V. He Was God-Fearing.
1. "The Lord is with him."

38. THE GREEN-EYED MONSTER

"And Saul eyed David from that day and forward."
I Sam. 18:9

Someone has said that jealousy and hate are cousins. Perhaps the relationship is closer—twins.

It was jealousy that:

1. Caused Cain to slay his brother Abel.
2. Caused Joseph's brothers to sell him into Egypt.
3. Caused Saul to seek David's life. Text.
4. Caused Herod to order the slaughter of the innocents of Bethlehem.
5. Caused the elder brother to regret the return of the prodigal.
6. Caused Jewish leaders to conspire the crucifixion of Jesus. "The world is gone after him."

39. ONLY A STEP

"There is but a step between me and death." *I Sam. 20:3*

I. It Is a Certain Step.
1. Every man must take it.
2. "The way of all the earth" (Josh. 23:14)

II. It Is a Solitary Step.
1. No human companionship possible
2. But the Christian can say: "Thou art with me."

III. It Is a Solemn Step.

IV. It Is a Final Step.

—John Porter

40. DON'T BE A FOOL

"I have played the fool."
I Sam. 26:21

How some have made fools of themselves:

1. By jealous rage (I Sam. 26:21)
2. By walking in the dark (Eccl. 2:14)
3. By atheism (Ps. 14:1)
4. By being pleasure mad (Eccl. 7:4)
5. By building on the sand (Matt. 7:26)
6. By unpreparedness (Matt. 25:3)
7. By living for self (Luke 12:20)

41. "HOW ARE YOU?"

"Art thou in health, my brother?" *II Sam. 20:9*

There may be a healthy soul in a sickly body. But often within a sound body there is an unsound spiritual condition.

I. CHARACTERISTICS OF A HEALTHY DISCIPLE
  1. A cheerful countenance
  2. A good appetite: "Hunger and thirst after righteousness."
  3. Moral strength
  4. Buoyant spirits

II. CAUSES OF SOUL SICKNESS
  1. Contagion; evil company
  2. Neglect

III. THE REMEDY
  1. Hurry to the Great Physician.
  2. "Wait upon the Lord . . . renew . . . strength."
  3. "Exercise thyself . . . unto godliness."

—F. J. Austin

42. AN UNDERSTANDING HEART

"Give therefore thy servant an understanding heart . . . , that I may discern between good and bad." *I Kings 3:9*

All of us have need to pray this prayer of Solomon. We need to pray for:

I. A BETTER UNDERSTANDING OF OURSELVES
  1. "Know thyself" (Socrates).
  2. "Let a man examine himself" (Paul).
  3. "I will chide no breather in the world but myself, against whom I know most faults" (Shakespeare).

II. A BETTER UNDERSTANDING OF OTHERS
  1. The Golden Rule
  2. Ezekiel: "I sat where they sat."

III. A BETTER UNDERSTANDING OF THE WORD OF GOD
  1. "Understandest thou what thou readest?"
  2. "Open thou mine eyes that I may behold wondrous things out of thy law."

IV. POWER TO DISCERN BETWEEN GOOD AND EVIL
  1. Many think evil is good and good is evil.
  2. Pray for discerning power.
  3. Pray for sensitivity.

43. THE MINISTRY OF MUSIC

"David spake to the chief of the Levites to appoint their brethren to be the singers with instruments of musick, psalteries and harps and cymbals, sounding, by lifting up the voice with joy." *I Chron. 15:16*

Some examples of the ministry of music:

1. A solo by a king (Ps. 23)
2. A duet in a prison (Acts 16:25)
3. An orchestra in the temple (II Chron. 5:12-13)
4. A chorus in heaven (Rev. 5:9)

44. CONSECRATION

"Who then is willing to consecrate his service this day unto the Lord?" *I Chron. 29:5*

Consecration implies:

1. Personal consecration: "Who?"
2. Voluntary consecration: "Who . . . is willing?"
3. Active consecration: "his service."
4. To God, not men: "unto the Lord."
5. Prompt consecration: "this day."

—T. K.

45. THE PRICE OF DIVINE FAVOR

"If my people, which are called by my name, shall humble themselves, and pray, and seek my face, and turn from their wicked ways; then will I hear from heaven, and will forgive their sin, and will heal their land."

II Chron. 7:14

I. THE COMPANY ADDRESSED
  1. "My people"
II. THE CONDITIONS REQUIRED
  1. Humiliation: "humble themselves"
  2. Intercession: "pray"
  3. Submission: "seek my face"
  4. Resignation: "turn from their wicked ways"
III. THE CONSEQUENCES ASSURED
  1. Prayers answered
  2. Sins forgiven
  3. Land healed

—Clarence M. Keen

46. A KING PRAYS

"Asa cried unto the Lord his God . . . ; help us, O Lord our God; for we rest on thee, and in thy name we go." *II Chron. 14:11*

Asa's prayer was:
1. Earnest—he cried.
2. Definite—"help us."
3. Personal—to God.
4. Believing—"we rest on thee."
5. Answered—verses 12-15.

47. BLESSED BE DRUDGERY

"I am doing a great work, so that I cannot come down."

Neh. 6:3

These words were uttered by a young reformer. Sought permission of Persian monarch to build walls of Jerusalem; request granted. Difficulties. Neighbors tried to dissuade him from his work. Reply in text.

I. NEHEMIAH'S WORK
  1. He was building for God.
II. NEHEMIAH'S TEMPTATIONS
  1. To give up the work
  2. To associate with evil companions
III. NEHEMIAH'S SECRET OF POWER
  1. He put everything into God's hands.
  2. He put God first.
  3. He put intelligence into his work.

Application: "Whatsoever thy hand findeth to do, do it with thy might."

—J. T. Heselton

48. ENDURING TRIAL

"In all this Job sinned not, nor charged God foolishly."

Job 1:22

In the hour of trial many fret and charge God foolishly.

1. We are apt to become impatient.—Even John the Baptist wondered if Jesus was the Messiah, because of his delays.

2. We are apt to become rebellious.

3. We are apt to despair, to give up hope.

4. We are apt to question God's love.

5. We are apt to question God's power.

Application: We should learn from Job not to charge God foolishly. "When he hath tried me, I shall come forth as gold."

49. THE ANSWER IS "YES!"

"If a man die, shall he live again?" *Job 14:14*

1. Nature answers, "Yes!"
2. Reason answers, "Yes!"
3. Revelation answers, "Yes!"
4. Jesus Christ answers, "Yes!"

50. MISERABLE COMFORTERS

"Miserable comforters are ye all." *Job 16:2*

Job's comforters deserved this epithet because:

1. They forgot that affliction is not necessarily punitive.

2. They did not discriminate between means and ends.

3. We shall never benefit a fel-

low man by casting the past in his teeth.

—J. S. Swan

51. WHAT A FRIEND!

"Acquaint now thyself with him, and be at peace: thereby good shall come unto thee." *Job 22:21*

Facts about Jesus, our Friend:

I. Royalty
   1. Son of God.
   2. Son of David.
   3. Prince of peace
   4. King of kings

II. Riches
   1. Paul speaks of His "unsearchable riches."
   2. "Though he was rich, yet for your sakes he became poor."

III. Constancy
   1. "Sticketh closer than a brother"
   2. "Lo, I am with you alway."
   3. "Same yesterday, and to day, and for ever"

IV. Candour
   1. "[A friend] that loveth . . . chasteneth."
   2. "Faithful are the wounds of a friend."

V. Love and Compassion
   1. "Greater love hath no man than this. . . ."
   2. Wept at Lazarus' tomb
   3. Compassion for the multitudes, as sheep without a shepherd

Application: "What a Friend we have in Jesus!" What kind of friend am I to Him?

52. THE BLESSEDNESS OF GODLINESS

"Blessed is the man. . . . His delight is in the law of the Lord. . . . And whatsoever he doeth shall prosper." *Ps. 1:1-3*

I. In Verse One the Godly Man Is Described by Negatives.
   1. "Walketh not"
   2. "Nor standeth"
   3. "Nor sitteth"

II. In Verse Two We Observe Some Positive Aspects of the Godly Man's Life.
   1. "His delight is in the law of the Lord."
   2. "In his law doth he meditate."

III. Verse Three Portrays Him as a Thing of Beauty and Utility.
   1. Taken from unfavorable soil and transplanted "by the rivers of water"
   2. Evergreen—"His leaf . . . shall not wither."
   3. Fruitful—"Bringeth forth his fruit in his season."
   4. Prospers

53. CHECK UP

"Commune with your own heart." *Ps. 4:4*

I. The Subjects of Self-Examination
   1. Our sins
   2. Our conversion
   3. Our principles
   4. Our pleasures
   5. Our prayers

II. The Manner in Which It Should Be Conducted
   1. Seriously
   2. Candidly
   3. By Bible standards
   4. Prayer for guidance

III. Advantages
   1. Self-knowledge will direct us in the use of God's grace.
   2. Self-knowledge will assist us in the performance of religious duties.
   3. Self-knowledge will guard us against temptation.

54. WHAT IS MAN?

"What is man, that thou art mindful of him?" *Ps. 8:4*

I. Creation's Masterpiece
   1. In the image of God
   2. Given dominion over other creatures

3. Entrusted with a soul

II. THE DWELLING PLACE OF GOD
1. Jesus: "We will . . . make our abode with him."
2. Paul: "Know ye not that ye are the temple of God?"
3. John: "If we love one another, God dwelleth in us."

III. MAN GOD'S AGENT IN THE WORLD
1. Jesus: "Go ye into all the world, and preach the gospel to every creature."
2. Paul: "We are ambassadors for Christ."
3. Paul: "Workers together with him."
4. God has no hands, feet, voice, but ours.

Questions:

Are we godly (God-like)?
Does the world see Jesus in us?
The Lord is mindful of us; are we mindful of him?

55. THE BETTER PATRIOTISM

"The wicked shall be turned into hell, and all the nations that forget God." *Ps. 9:17*

I. THE TRUE PATRIOT IS A COMPATRIOT. (His patriotism is social. It takes others into account.)
1. Moses: "Save these people . . . or blot me out"
2. Nehemiah's heavy heart
3. Esther
4. Paul: "I could wish that myself were accursed for . . . my brethren, . . . who are Israelites."
5. Jesus: tears over Jerusalem; death for others

II. THE TRUE AMERICAN PATRIOT IS CHRISTIAN.
1. Whatever greatness America knows is traceable to the Christian principles and purposes of the founding fathers.
2. Our great historic documents are permeated with biblical atmosphere: Declaration of Independence, Constitution, Lincoln's Address at Gettysburg.
3. National anthem: "May the Heaven-rescued land praise the Power that hath made and preserved us a nation."
4. Motto on coins: "In God We Trust."
5. "A 30 per-cent Christian can't be a 100 per-cent American."

Application:

Beware of our dire fate if we forget God. Text.

"The highways of history are strewn with the wreckage of nations that forgot God."

56. THE PATH OF LIFE

"Thou wilt shew me the path of life." *Ps. 16:11*

Facts about the path of life:

1. It is a straight path. (Prov. 4:25-27; Heb. 12:13.)
2. It is a narrow path. (Matt. 7:13-14.)
3. It is an upward path. (Prov. 15:24; Isa. 40:31.)
4. It is an old path. (Jer. 6:16.)
5. It is a pleasant path. (Prov. 3:17.)
6. It is a light path. (Prov. 4:18.)
7. It leads to a glorious city. (Ps. 107:7.)

—*Curiosities of the Bible*

57. SINS OF PRESUMPTION

"Keep back thy servant . . . from presumptuous sins; let them not have dominion over me." *Ps. 19:13*

Sins may roughly be classified under four heads: ignorance, infirmity, negligence, and presumption. The latter are the most offensive.

What are sins of presumption?

I. TO TREAT UNCONCERNEDLY OUR SECRET FAULTS

1. "Be sure your sin will find you out."
2. "As [a man] thinketh in his heart, so is he."
3. "Keep thy heart with all diligence; for out of it are the issues of life."
4. "Of the abundance of the heart the mouth speaketh."
5. "Thou God seest me."

II. To Treat Lightly the Beginnings of Habit

1. "The trouble with little sins is they don't stay little."
2. "Habit is a cable. We weave a thread for it each day, and at last we cannot break it."

III. To Face Eternity Without Preparation

1. Foolish Virgins
2. Man who built upon the sand
3. All who say, or think, "It can't happen to me."

IV. To Think There Is Another Chance After Death

1. "[The wicked] shall go . . . into everlasting punishment." Jesus.
2. Dives and Lazarus
3. "He that is unjust, let him be. . . ." (Revelation.)

—W. L. Watkinson

58. FLING OUT THE BANNER!

"In the name of our God we will set up our banners." *Ps. 20:5*

I. Where Should the Church's Banners Be Set Up?

1. An easy answer to the question is to ask another, "Where not?"
2. Jesus said: "Go . . . into all the world."

II. When?

1. Immediately. We have lost too much time already.
2. "The king's business require[th] haste."

III. Why?

1. The Christian must share the blessings of salvation.
2. The world needs the Christian gospel. It is the one and only panacea for the world's ills.

IV. How?

1. The enormity of the task is not greater than the strength of the omnipotent God who commands it.
2. "With God all things are possible."

59. LOVE FOR THE CHURCH

"Lord, I have loved the habitation of thy house, and the place where thine honour dwelleth."

Ps. 26:8

There are many good reasons for loving the house of God.

I. It Is the Particular Place Where God Manifests His Presence

1. "The Lord is in his holy temple."
2. "I saw . . . the Lord, . . . high and lifted up."

II. The Appointed Place for Prayer and Keeping Tryst with God.

1. "My house shall be called the house of prayer."
2. The apostles attended prayer meeting. (Acts 3:1.)

III. For Most of Us It Is a Place of Sacred Memories and Hallowed Traditions.

1. Forefathers were churchgoers.
2. Memories of our youth and youthful associations.
3. Memories of our acceptance of Christ; baptism; church affiliation.

IV. It Is the Gateway to Heaven

1. "None other but the house of God, and . . . the gate of heaven." Jacob.

V. The Church Offers the Finest Fraternity on Earth.

1. Despite the few hypocrites, worldly minded, and insincere people who attend, the church still has the finest people on earth.
2. Clubs, fraternities, and social organizations have their place and value, but they are incomparable to the Church.

60. THE CONQUEST OF FEAR

"The Lord is my light and my salvation; whom shall I fear?" *Ps. 27:1*

I. SHALL WE FEAR THE LAW?
II. SHALL WE FEAR SATAN?
III. SHALL WE FEAR AFFLICTION?
IV. SHALL WE FEAR DEATH?

61. GOD BLESS AMERICA!

"Blessed is the nation whose God is the Lord." *Ps. 33:12*

I. WHAT DO WE MEAN BY SINGING, OR SAYING, OR PRAYING, "GOD BLESS AMERICA"?
   1. Too many are thinking of material prosperity only.
   2. We have need to avoid materialism and selfishness in praying this prayer.

II. "GOD BLESS AMERICA" WITH SPIRITUAL BLESSINGS.
   1. We need a recovery of lost values.
   2. We need the "Faith of Our Fathers."
   3. We need a rebirth of appreciation of God's day, God's Book, God's house, and God's will.

III. "GOD BLESS AMERICA!" PERHAPS IT WOULD BE WELL TO PRAY, "GOD SAVE AMERICA!"
   1. From materialism, selfishness, drunkenness, gluttony, graft, greed, corruption in high places
   2. A man's foes can be they of his own household.

IV. "GOD BLESS AMERICA!" THE CHURCH IS THE CHANNEL THROUGH WHICH GOD BLESSES THE WORLD.
   1. The measure of your church loyalty is the measure of your patriotism.
   2. "A 30 per-cent Christian can't be a 100 per-cent American."
   3. We should not ask God to bless America if we are doing nothing ourselves to this end.

62. THE KEEPING POWER OF GOD

"The righteous cry, and the Lord heareth, and delivereth them out of all their troubles. . . . None of them that trust in him shall be desolate." *Ps. 34:17, 22*

The Lord
1. Heareth the prayerful (verse 17).
2. Saveth the contrite (verse 18).
3. Delivereth the Righteous (verse 19).
4. Keepeth the strengthless (verse 20).
5. Redeemeth the obedient (verse 22).

—*The Christian*

63. DELIVERANCE FROM FEAR

"I sought the Lord, and he heard me, and delivered me from all my fears." *Ps. 34:4*

I. THE FEAR OF WANT
   1. "God will provide."
   2. "I shall not want."
   3. "Behold the fowls: . . . your heavenly Father feedeth them. Are ye not much better than they?"

II. THE FEAR OF ENEMIES
   1. National: "Blessed is the nation whose God is the Lord."
   2. Personal: "The Lord is my helper, and I will not fear

what man shall do unto me."

III. THE FEAR OF SPEAKING
1. "He spake boldly in the name of the Lord Jesus."
2. "We cannot but speak the things which we have seen and heard."

IV. THE FEAR OF PHYSICAL DEATH
1. Stephen's example: Acts 7:54-60.
2. Paul's exclamation: "O death, where is thy sting?"

64. THE SIN OF FRETFULNESS

"Fret not thyself because of evildoers." *Ps. 37:1*

I. THE SIN OF FRETFULNESS
1. A sin against ourselves: destroys peace of mind; fosters bitterness, harshness, faultfinding
2. A sin against others
3. A sin against God

II. THE CAUSES
1. Envy
2. Covetousness
3. Want of faith in God

III. THE CURE
1. Look on the bright side. There always is one.
2. Look not merely at the present, but into the future.
3. Have faith in God.

—J. Scilley

65. ON BEING DUMB

"I was dumb with silence, I held my peace, even from good." *Ps. 39:2*

The average church has its full quota of dumb people. Not dumb in the sense of ignorance, or lack of education, or natural stupidity, but in the sense of being tight-lipped when it comes to using the voice for God.

I. SOME PROFESSING CHRISTIANS DO NOT USE THEIR VOICES IN THE PRAISE OF GOD.
1. Ready to speak up in praise of an athlete, a movie star, a politician, or a patent medicine, but rarely talk out for Christ and the church.
2. Some fail to join in the singing of hymns of praise.
3. "One reason some people don't talk much about their religion is they don't have much to talk about."

II. SOME ARE DUMB WITH SILENCE WHEN IT COMES TO SAYING WORDS OF APPRECIATION.
1. Appreciation is a "fine art."
2. A beautiful habit, or quality, to be generous with words of praise.

III. SOME ARE DUMB WHEN IT COMES TO ADMONITION.
1. A word of warning may be as love-filled as a word of praise.
2. Isaiah: "Cry aloud, spare not, lift up thy voice like a trumpet, and shew my people their transgression."
3. The duty of Christians to break silence, and speak out against evils of every description—strong drink, gambling, social evils, Sabbath desecration, and sin in every other form.

66. MEDITATION IN THE FIRELIGHT

"While I was musing the fire burned." *Ps. 39:3*

I. SOME EXCELLENT SUBJECTS FOR QUIET MEDITATION
1. The character of God
2. His providential dealings
3. The plan of salvation
4. Our relation to God
5. Our future life

II. BENEFITS OF MEDITATION
1. Faith is inspired and increased.
2. Hope is more firmly anchored.

3. Love for God and man is shed abroad in our hearts.

67. WHY WAIT?

"And now, Lord, what wait I for? my hope is in thee." *Ps. 39:7*

Millions honestly and sincerely intend coming to Christ. It is simply that they never get around to it. The opportune moment never seems to arrive.

Why do they wait?

I. NOT BECAUSE THE CHURCH DOES NOT WANT THEM
   1. In the name of Christ every church opens wide its doors, makes free a place, and in the name of the Lord says, "Welcome."
   2. "There is joy in the presence of the angels of God over one sinner that repenteth."

II. NOT BECAUSE TIME WILL MAKE A DECISION EASIER
   1. The reverse is true. Statistics prove it.
   2. "Now is the accepted time. . . ."

III. NOT BECAUSE THE PROCESS OF SALVATION IS DIFFICULT
   1. Jesus invited the fishermen: "Follow me." "And they straightway left their nets, and followed him." It's as simple as that.
   2. "All the fitness he requireth is to feel your need of him."

IV. NOT BECAUSE IT IS SAFE TO DO SO
   1. Solomon: "Boast not thyself of to morrow."
   2. Jesus: "Watch. . . . Ye know neither the day nor the hour."

68. DELIVERANCE

"He brought me up also out of an horrible pit, out of the miry clay, and set my feet upon a rock, and established my goings. And he hath put a new song in my mouth, even praise unto our God: many shall see it, and fear, and shall trust in the Lord."

Ps. 40:2-3

I. SORROW, TROUBLE: "horrible pit" (Helplessness)

II. SALVATION: "He brought me up." (Hope)

III. SAFETY: "set my feet upon a rock" (Holiness)

IV. SONGS: "put a new song in my mouth" (Happiness)

V. SERVICE: "Many shall see it, and fear." (Helping others)

—C. Edwards

69. PANTING FOR THE WATER BROOKS

"As the hart panteth after the water brooks, so panteth my soul after thee, O God." *Ps. 42:1*

In Bible times, as now, deer were hunted by men and dogs. Chased through mountains and wildernesses, foaming, steaming, lathered, the hart panted for the cool water brooks—and peace.

I. HUMAN LIFE HAS SOME OF THE ASPECTS OF "THE CHASE."
   1. Sinister forces ever on our trail, seeking our spiritual destruction
   2. Satan ever alert, seeking whom he may devour
   3. Many of us, weary in well-doing, long for security and peace.

II. "THE FOUNTAIN LIES OPEN."
   1. "Ho, every one that thirsteth, come!"
   2. "Whosoever will, let him take the water of life freely."
   3. "Blessed are they which do hunger and thirst after righteousness."

III. A STRANGE PHENOMENON
   1. "They have forsaken me the fountain of living waters, and hewed them out cisterns, broken cisterns, that can hold no water."

2. Some prefer the stagnant cesspools of sin to the sparkling, effervescent, life-giving water of life.

70. SPIRITUAL DEPRESSION

"Why art thou cast down, O my soul? and why art thou disquieted within me? hope thou in God, for I shall yet praise him, who is the health of my countenance, and my God." *Ps. 42:11*

I. SOME CAUSES OF SPIRITUAL DEPRESSION
   1. The burden of sin.
   2. The wickedness of the world (Elijah)
   3. Unanswered prayer
   4. Ill health
   5. Bereavement
   6. Misfortune

II. THE WAY OUT—"HOPE THOU IN GOD."
   1. "Have faith in God."
   2. "Count your many blessings."
   3. Review the promises of God.
   4. The Christian's troubles are but temporary—"I shall yet praise him."

71. THINK AND THANK

"We have thought of thy lovingkindness, O God, in the midst of thy temple." *Ps. 48:9*

I. "COUNT YOUR MANY BLESSINGS."
   1. It can't be done, but the exercise is profitable.
   2. It is our duty to meditate on the goodness of God.

II. "NAME THEM ONE BY ONE."
   1. Some think of their blessings en masse, in the abstract, all of them in general.
   2. We should also be specific. Particularize.

III. "AND IT WILL SURPRISE YOU."
   1. Your wealth of blessings will astonish you.
   2. "Oh that men would praise the Lord for his goodness, and for his wonderful works to the children of men!"

IV. "WHAT THE LORD HATH DONE."
   1. The glory belongs to God.
   2. "What hath God wrought!"
   3. "Praise God from whom all blessings flow."

72. THE PREDOMINANT GOD

"The mighty God, even the Lord, hath spoken, and called the earth from the rising of the sun unto the going down thereof. . . . And the heavens shall declare his righteousness: for God is judge himself." *Ps. 50:1, 6*

God's predominance is evident in:

1. His power (verse 1)
2. His perfection (verse 2)
3. His proclamation (verse 3*a*)
4. His purpose (verses 3*b*, 4*a*)
5. His proposal (verse 5)
6. His promise (verse 6)

—O. L. Huffman

73. WITHOUT A GOD

"The fool hath said in his heart, There is no God." *Ps. 53:1*

The fool has:

1. No God in his heart (verse 1)
2. No good by his hand (verse 3).
3. No glory in his future (verse 6)

74. "THE SLOUGH OF DESPOND"

"Oh, that I had wings like a dove! for then would I fly away, and be at rest." *Ps. 55:6*

Bunyan tells of a man who set forth in quest of heaven. He didn't get far before he bogged down in the "Slough of Despond." Most of us, sooner or later, find ourselves similarly situated. David was no exception. Text.

I. OTHER BIBLE CHARACTERS HAVE HAD THEIR PERIODS OF DESPONDENCY.
   1. Elijah under the juniper tree
   2. Job: "My soul is weary of my life."
   3. Jeremiah: "Oh, that I had in the wilderness a lodging place of wayfaring men," etc.
   4. Paul: thorn in the flesh
   5. John the Baptist: "Art thou he . . . ?"

II. THE WAY OUT
   1. "When the outlook is dark, try the uplook."
   2. "Looking unto Jesus the author and finisher of our faith"
   3. Pray not for the "wings of a dove" with which to escape from reality.
   4. Pray for the strength of the eagle.
   5. "They that wait upon the Lord shall renew their strength."

75. TRUST HIM

"Trust in him at all times."
Ps. 62:8

Trust him:
1. For guidance (Ps. 37:5)
2. For strength (Isa. 26:4)
3. In the dark (Isa. 50:10)
4. When he permits affliction (Job 13:15)
5. The Lord knoweth them that trust him. (Nah. 1:7.)

—E. A. H.

76. LIP SERVICE

"My mouth shall praise thee with joyful lips." *Ps. 63:5*

1. Smiling lips—man the only creature of God that can smile.

2. Laughing lips—thank God for fun. "A merry heart doeth good like a medicine."

3. Singing lips—sing away the clouds and sing joy and peace into your own heart, and into the hearts of others.

4. Praying lips—how thankful we ought to be for lips to speak the message of the heart to God!

5. Witnessing lips—our sacred duty and privilege to declare the goodness of God and win others to discipleship.

77. WITNESSING FOR CHRIST

"Come and hear, all ye that fear God, and I will declare what he hath done for my soul."
Ps. 66:16

I. WHAT GOD DOES FOR THE SOULS OF HIS PEOPLE
   1. Pardons sin
   2. Regenerates
   3. Gives victory over temptation
   4. Gives answers to prayer

II. WHY CHRISTIANS SHOULD BEAR TESTIMONY
   1. Out of gratitude to God
   2. From a desire to help others
   3. A means of self-improvement

78. THE GROWTH OF THE CHURCH

"There shall be an handful of corn in the earth upon the top of the mountains; the fruit thereof shall shake like Lebanon."
Ps. 72:16

I. THE DIM OUTLOOK FOR THE PRIMITIVE CHURCH
   1. No resources
   2. Disciples uneducated; poor; unorganized
   3. The opposition was powerful.

II. THE STUPENDOUS RESULTS
   1. Adherents now number one third the population of the globe.
   2. Organized for service
   3. Vast property holdings, dedicated to Christ
   4. Educational and benevolent institutions
   5. Missionary endeavors

6. Millions saved for time and eternity

III. The Secret of the Church's Growth
1. Christ's followers have scattered the seed.
2. God gave the increase.

79. THE VALUES OF WORSHIP

"It is good for me to draw near to God." *Ps. 73:28*

I. Worship Is an Aid to Physical Health.
1. The Christian understands his body to be the temple of God, and should care for it accordingly.
2. Christianity fosters cleanliness, sanitation, hygiene, the science of healing.

II. Worship Breaks Down Social Barriers and Exalts Human Equality.
1. "The rich and poor meet together: the Lord is the maker of them all."
2. No such thing as an "exclusive" church

III. Worship Helps a Man Locate Himself.
1. The maze of pathways and the confusion of tongues, philosophies, and ideologies bewilder us.
2. The mariner must consult his chart, the tourist his road map, the builder his plans.
3. Worship gives man a sense of direction.
4. Worship enlightens the conscience; throws a beam of light upon the pathway; helps man discriminate between vice and virtue.

IV. Worship Puts a Man Into Touch with God.
1. A means of communication
2. A two-way talking instrument
3. Worship makes a man a citizen of two worlds.

80. SECRET SINS

"Thou hast set our iniquities before thee, our secret sins in the light of thy countenance." *Ps. 90:8*

I. Sin Naturally Seeks Concealment.
1. The first impulse of the first sinners, Adam and Eve, was to hide from God.
2. Many prefer darkness "because their deeds [are] evil."

II. Sin Cannot Be Hidden from God.
1. "Thou God seest me."
2. "The eyes of the Lord are in every place, beholding the evil and the good."
3. Text

III. Sins Usually Are Apparent to Others.
1. "Be sure your sin will find you out."
2. Nathan to David: "Thou art the man."

IV. Though Sins Cannot Be Hidden, They Can Be Covered.
1. Ps. 32:1
2. Ps. 85:2

81. LIKE A CEDAR IN LEBANON

"The righteous shall flourish like the palm tree: he shall grow like a cedar in Lebanon." *Ps. 92:12*

I. The Cedar Grows Downward (sends taproot deep, seeking hidden springs, and twining about rocks for anchorage).
1. Paul urged the Ephesians to be "rooted and grounded in love."
2. Stanley Jones: "Before we can go farther, we must go deeper."

II. The Cedar Grows Upward (sometimes 150 feet).
1. Christians walk on the earth, but their heads should be above the clouds.
2. J. G. Holland: "God give us

men; tall, sun-crowned, who live above the fog."

III. THE CEDAR GROWS OUTWARD (beauty, shade, shelter).
  1. Christian lives should be beautiful, useful.

IV. THE CEDAR GROWS ONWARD (noted for longevity).
  1. The Christian is a perennial, evergreen, "instant in season, out of season."
  2. The Christian is immortal.

82. THE PEOPLE OF GOD

"He is our God; and we are the people of his pasture." *Ps. 95:7*

I. A SAVED PEOPLE (verse 1)
II. A SINGING PEOPLE (verse 2)
III. A WORSHIPING PEOPLE (verse 6)
IV. A SHEPHERDED PEOPLE (verse 7)

83. THE ESSENTIALS OF WORSHIP

"O worship the Lord in the beauty of holiness." *Ps. 96:9*

1. Prayer is the heartbeat of worship.
2. Peace is the soul of worship.
3. Penitence is the approach of worship.
4. Prejudice is the obstacle of worship.
5. Perilous is it to neglect worship.
6. Precious is the experience of worship.
7. Praise is the exultation of worship.
8. Patience is the reward of worship.
9. Personality is the character impress of worship.
10. Prophecy is the cradle of worship.

—Walter D. Mehrling

84. BUNDLES OF BENEFITS

"Bless the Lord, O my soul, and forget not all his benefits." *Ps. 103:2*

I. "WHO FORGIVETH ALL THINE INIQUITIES" (verse 3)
II. "WHO HEALETH ALL THY DISEASES" (verse 3)
III. "WHO REDEEMETH THY LIFE FROM DESTRUCTION" (verse 4)
IV. "WHO CROWNETH THEE WITH LOVINGKINDNESS AND TENDER MERCIES" (verse 4)
V. "WHO SATISFIETH THY MOUTH WITH GOOD THINGS" (verse 5)
VI. THE RENEWAL OF YOUTH (verse 5)

85. NATURAL LAW IN THE SPIRITUAL WORLD

"O Lord, how manifold are thy works! in wisdom hast thou made them all." *Ps. 104:24*

I. THE TELEGRAPH AND CABLE: "What hath God wrought!"
II. THE AIRPLANE: "They shall mount up with wings as eagles."
III. THE PHONOGRAPH (perpetuating voices and music): "He being dead yet speaketh."
IV. THE WIRELESS AND THE RADIO: "Whither shall I go from thy spirit?"
V. TELEVISION: "The eyes of the Lord are in every place."
VI. THE ATOMIC BOMB: "He uttered his voice, the earth melted."

86. SAY SO

"Let the redeemed of the Lord say so." *Ps. 107:2*

I. WHAT THE REDEEMED ARE URGED TO DO—BEAR TESTIMONY
  1. "Ye are witnesses."
  2. We are not required to be eloquent, to use flawless rhetoric, perfect diction.
  3. Ecclesiastical terms not necessary
  4. We are to witness for

Christ in a natural, conversational way.

II. WHAT THE REDEEMED ARE TO SAY—"SAY SO"
  1. Their personal redemption
  2. The power of Christ to redeem all
  3. If truly redeemed, we can't keep silent. "Of the abundance of the heart the mouth speaketh."

III. WHERE THE REDEEMED ARE TO "SAY SO"
  1. In the home; social circle; where employed
  2. In the house of God
  3. Where not?

Application:

Gospel doesn't need defenders, but witnesses.

Paul: "I am not ashamed of the gospel of Christ."

87. ON KEEPING PROMISES

"I will pay my vows unto the Lord now in the presence of all his people." *Ps. 116:14*

A religious vow should be considered as binding, or more so, as signatures to contracts, legal documents, or other forms of pledges. Yet many make light of their sacred vows, for instance:

I. CHURCH MEMBERSHIP VOWS
  1. Vows taken solemnly in the presence of God and the church
  2. Résumé of questions asked candidates for membership

II. BAPTISMAL VOWS
  1. Taken by parents on behalf of infants
  2. Taken by adults on their own behalf

III. MARITAL VOWS
  1. If the vow to "love, honor, and cherish" were kept by husbands and wives, the divorce mills would cease to grind, and domestic-relations courts could be abandoned.
  2. Broken hearts and broken homes result from broken marriage vows.

IV. FINANCIAL PLEDGES AND HONEST DEBTS
  1. "Better is it that thou shouldest not vow, than . . . vow and not pay."
  2. "Will a man rob God?" Instances
  3. "Some pay their dues when due;
     Some when overdue;
     Some never do;
     How do you do?"

88. THE CHRISTIAN SABBATH

"This is the day which the Lord hath made; we will rejoice and be glad in it." *Ps. 118:24*

I. THE LORD'S DAY
  1. A day of rest from physical toil
  2. A day set apart for the public worship of God
  3. A day for promoting our best and eternal interests
  4. A day designed for sacred enjoyment
  5. A day for perpetuating religion in the world

II. OUR DUTY WITH REGARD TO THE LORD'S DAY
  1. Thank God for this wise and gracious provision for our good.
  2. Rejoice in it as a type of the eternal Sabbath.
  3. Remember to keep it holy.

89. A PROSPEROUS CHURCH

"O Lord, I beseech thee, send now prosperity." *Ps. 118:25*

A church is prosperous when it has:

1. A spiritual membership
2. A learning membership
3. A zealous membership
4. A working membership
5. A soul-winning membership
6. A missionary-minded membership

7. A praying membership
8. A paying membership

90. THE CHRISTIAN'S SATISFACTION IN GOD

"Thou art my portion, O Lord." *Ps. 119:57*

God is:
1. A suitable portion
2. A satisfying portion
3. A universally accessible portion
4. An ever-present portion
5. An unchanging portion
6. An everlasting portion

91. THE BIBLE BETTER THAN MONEY

"The law of thy mouth is better unto me than thousands of gold and silver." *Ps. 119:72*

The Bible is better than money:

I. BECAUSE IT GIVES US BETTER FOOD
   1. Money cannot buy food for the soul; the Bible does provide this in unstinted measure.
   2. "Man shall not live by bread alone."

II. BECAUSE IT GIVES US BETTER RAIMENT
   1. Money can buy fine garments, but none for the soul.
   2. The Robe of Righteousness.

III. BECAUSE IT GIVES US BETTER FRIENDS
   1. The friends money buys are transient, as with the Prodigal.
   2. The Bible puts us into touch with the noblest and choicest spirits among men and angels.

IV. BECAUSE IT GIVES US A BETTER HOME
   1. Money can't buy for us the "house not made with hands, eternal in the heavens."
   2. The Bible has the key that unlocks Heaven's gate.

—J. Dunlop

92. THE BIBLE A LAMP

"Thy word is a lamp unto my feet, and a light unto my path." *Ps. 119:105*

1. Is a guiding light
2. Is a dependable light
3. Is a penetrating light
4. Illuminates the tomb

93. THE LIGHT OF SACRED STORY

"The entrance of thy words giveth light." *Ps. 119:130*

The Bible throws light:
1. On the nature of God
2. On the character and personality of Christ
3. On the functions of the Holy Spirit
4. On the nature and awfulness of sin
5. On the Atonement
6. On what lies beyond the grave

94. PEACE OF MIND

"Great peace have they which love thy law: and nothing shall offend them." *Ps. 119:165*

I. THE ESSENTIAL CONDITION INVOLVED
   1. Love for the teachings of God and his Word
   2. A positive attitude; not just respect, submission

II. THE SECRET OF PEACE OF MIND
   1. The psalmist was a psychiatrist.
   2. Jesus: "My peace I give unto you: not as the world giveth. . . ."
   3. It is the peace "which passeth all understanding."
   4. The peace the world can neither give nor take away
   5. Love for the laws of God would bring soul peace; domestic peace; world peace and good will.

III. "NOTHING SHALL OFFEND" THOSE WHO LOVE THE LAWS OF GOD.
1. Not easily peeved; do not fly off on a tangent; are not quitters
2. Not offended at difficult scriptures
3. Do not stumble at God's providential dealings

95. THE DIVINE KEEPER

"The Lord is thy keeper." *Ps. 121:5*

The Lord is:

I. AN OMNIPOTENT KEEPER ("Made heaven and earth." Verse 2.)
II. A SURE KEEPER ("He will not suffer thy foot to be moved." Verse 3.)
III. A VIGILANT KEEPER ("He that keepeth thee will not slumber." Verse 3.)
IV. A TENDER KEEPER ("The Lord is thy shade upon thy right hand." Verse 5.)
V. A HOLY KEEPER ("The Lord shall preserve [keep] thee from all evil." Verse 7.)
VI. A SPIRITUAL KEEPER ("He shall preserve thy *soul*." Verse 7.)
VII. AN ETERNAL KEEPER ("The Lord shall preserve . . . even for evermore." Verse 8.)

—*The Christian*

96. YOUR FATHER'S HOUSE

"I was glad when they said unto me, Let us go into the house of the Lord." *Ps. 122:1*

This is your Father's house. Therefore:

1. Enter expectantly.
2. Feel at home.
3. Breathe prayerfully.
4. Relax restfully.
5. Worship soulfully.
6. Greet others cordially.
7. Leave thoughtfully.
8. Come again soon.

97. IN QUEST OF HAPPINESS

"Happy is that people, whose God is the Lord." *Ps. 144:15*

I. HAPPINESS IS THE UNIVERSAL QUEST.
1. Some seek it in adventure, wealth, sports, alcohol, immorality, gluttony, etc.
2. Perverted forms of religion
3. Asceticism

II. THE TEXT HAS THE ANSWER.
1. Happiness results when the soul is set free from the thralldom of sin.
2. God offers peace of mind and heart.
3. The Christian has a satisfying philosophy of life. "All things work together."
4. The Christian finds happiness in the fellowship of God's people.
5. The Christian finds happiness in doing the Lord's work.
6. "A task worth doing and friends worth having make life worth living."

III. THE CHRISTIAN'S HAPPINESS IS PERPETUAL.
1. "In thy presence is fulness of joy; at thy right hand there are pleasures for evermore." Ps. 16:11.
2. "God shall wipe away all tears." Rev. 7:17.

Application: "If ye know these things, happy are ye if ye do them."

98. WHEN SINNERS ENTICE

"My son, if sinners entice thee, consent thou not." *Prov. 1:10*

I. THE SALUTATION: "MY SON"
1. This could be Solomon's tender advice to his own son.
2. The voice of mature wisdom to all young people

II. "IF SINNERS ENTICE THEE"
1. "If." Perhaps a better word would be "when."
2. Sinners are busy with enticements.
3. Sin is portrayed as harmless, pleasurable.
4. Satan disguises himself as "an angel of light."

III. "CONSENT THOU NOT"
1. After all, you make the decision.
2. No sin in being tempted. Jesus was tempted.
3. "Yield not to temptation,
For yielding is sin."
4. "You can't prevent birds flying over your head, but you can keep them from building nests in your hair."

Application: "My soul, be on thy guard."

99. LEARNING FROM ANTS

"Go to the ant, thou sluggard; consider her ways, and be wise."
Prov. 6:6

I. A LESSON IN INDUSTRY
(Always at work)

II. A LESSON IN PERSEVERANCE
(When an ant hill is destroyed, the ants start all over.)

III. A LESSON IN UNITY
(Work together. Each has a task.)

IV. A LESSON IN PRUDENCE
(In summer they prepare for winter.)

100. SIN A BOOMERANG

"But he that sinneth against me wrongeth his own soul."
Prov. 8:36

I. OTHER SCRIPTURES SUBSTANTIATE THIS TEXT.
1. Jesus: "Do men gather grapes of thorns, or figs of thistles?"
2. Paul: "Whatsoever a man soweth, that shall he also reap."
3. Paul: "The wages of sin is death."
4. E. Stanley Jones: "You can't break the Commandments; they break you."

II. THE SINNER WRONGS HIMSELF.
1. When profane and vulgar. He forfeits respect of refined people, alienates friends, endangers his own soul.
2. When he does not tell the truth. It doesn't take long for associates to "get your number."
3. When he forsakes God's holy altars. The church and the pastor miss him, but he is the main loser. Illustration: Thomas.
4. Every conceivable type of sin reacts to the sorrow of the one committing it.

Application: "Be sure your sin will find you out."

101. THE WISDOM OF SOUL WINNING

"He that winneth souls is wise."
Prov. 11:30

I. THE SOUL WINNER HAS THE INNER SATISFACTION OF HAVING PAID A DEBT.
1. Through someone's efforts we have been brought to Christ. We are thus in debt.
2. We repay the debt by helping another to a knowledge of sins forgiven and right relations with God.

II. THERE IS SATISFACTION IN TURNING OTHERS TO RIGHTEOUSNESS.
1. We are saving them *from* something as well as *to* something.
2. James: "He which converteth the sinner from the error of his way shall save a soul from death, and shall hide a multitude of sins."
3. It is better to prevent disease than cure it; it is better to win souls to right-

eousness than save them after years of sinning.

III. The Soul Winner's Best Reward Is in the Future.
1. Dan. 12:3. "They that turn many to righeousness [shall shine] as the stars for ever and ever."
2. Heaven will be more enjoyable if we may greet souls whom we have won to Christ.

Application:

"Will there be any stars in my crown?"

"Will I have sheaves to lay at the Master's feet?"

102. THE HIGH COST OF SIN

"The way of transgressors is hard." *Prov. 13:15*

Things that make the way of the transgressor hard:
1. The loss of a good conscience
2. The loss of character
3. The loss of usefulness
4. The loss of the soul

—Richard Newton

103. FELLOWSHIP WITH FOOLS

"A companion of fools shall be destroyed." *Prov. 13:20*

We are cautioned about calling others "fools." However, the Bible calls certain persons fools, so fools they must be.

I. Fools of the Bible
1. The Atheist. "The fool hath said in his heart, There is no God" (Ps. 14:1). Only a fool would say such a thing.
2. Unteachable people. "Fools despise wisdom and instruction" (Prov. 1:7). Many have closed minds, are opinionated, do not want truth.
3. Those who treat sin lightly. "Fools make a mock at sin" (Prov. 14:9). Many speak jokingly of hell, as though it were a myth.
4. Those who make no preparation to meet God. The five foolish virgins; the foolish man who built upon the sand.
5. The self-worshiper. The rich barn builder. "Thou fool, this night thy soul shall be required of thee" (Luke 12:20).

II. Text
1. Fools drag others down to their level.
2. Stay away from fools.

104. MAKING LIGHT OF SIN

"Fools make a mock at sin." *Prov. 14:9*

I. Men Are So Accustomed to Sin They Come to Treat It Lightly.
1. It is so common that their hearts are hardened.
2. It is so universal that they are never startled.

II. Men Treat Sin Lightly Because It So Often Is Intertwined with the Good.

III. Men Are Tempted to Treat Sin Lightly Because It Veils Its Consequences with Such Consummate Skill.

IV. Many Make Light of Sin Because No One Knows Sin's Power till He Resists It.

—G. H. Morrison

105. SELF-DISCIPLINE

"He that ruleth his spirit [is better] than he that taketh a city." *Prov. 16:32*

Alexander wept because there were no more worlds to conquer, yet he died a drunkard at thirty-three. He had failed in the conquest of self.

The Christian should be a shining example of self-discipline. He should discipline:

I. His Human Nature
1. He should circumscribe his

desires and keep his passions within bounds.
2. Paul: "I keep under my body, and bring it into subjection."

II. HIS MIND AND HEART
1. "As he thinketh in his heart, so is he."
2. Man should be master of his fate, captain of his soul.

III. HIS EMOTIONS, ESPECIALLY ANGER
1. Uncontrolled anger is emotional insanity.
2. "A fit of rage" is well named. It is a "fit."
3. Text

IV. HIS SENSE OF DUTY
1. Self-denial (Matt. 16:24)

---

106. MONEY ISN'T EVERYTHING

"A good name is rather to be chosen than great riches, and loving favour rather than silver and gold." *Prov. 22:1*

Some things to be preferred above riches:

1. A good name
2. A happy home
3. Peace of mind
4. Salvation, and a home in heaven

---

107. HUMAN EQUALITY

"The rich and poor meet together: the Lord is the maker of them all." *Prov. 22:2*

The rich and poor meet on common ground:

1. In the sameness of their origin
2. In the construction and modification of their persons
3. In the calamitous consequences of the fall
4. In the gracious arrangements of redeeming mercy
5. In the field of mutual dependence and usefulness
6. In the infirmities and miseries to which humanity is liable
7. Within the silent precincts of the tomb
8. Before the judgment seat of Christ

---

108. GOLDEN APPLES

"A word fitly spoken is like apples of gold in pictures of silver." *Prov. 25:11*

Some words "fitly spoken":

1. A word of greeting and good cheer
2. A word of comfort and encouragement
3. A word of love and appreciation
4. A word of warning and admonition
5. A good word for Christ and the Church

---

109. WHEN PRIDE IS SIN

"A man's pride shall bring him low: but honour shall uphold the humble in spirit." *Prov. 29:23*

There are some forms of commendable pride: a good name, a garden, neatness and cleanliness of home, personal appearance, children making good in the world, etc.

On the other hand, God condemns certain forms of pride:

I. RACE PRIDE
1. The mere fact that one's skin is of a different color doesn't make him better than another.
2. Paul: "[God] hath made of one blood all nations."

II. FACE PRIDE
1. The mere possession of beautiful features and figures does not warrant pride.
2. The devil's "heart was lifted up because of [his] beauty"

III. PLACE PRIDE
1. The place where you live doesn't make you better or worse than another.
2. Your place in the social world, financial world, political or cultural world, of little importance.

3. Judeans thought their locale made them better than Samaritans, Galileans, etc.
4. Some city people have a superiority complex.
5. Some think their church, their denomination, or their ecclesiastical heritage makes them better than others.

110. THE MILLS OF GOD GRIND SLOWLY, BUT—

"Because sentence against an evil work is not executed speedily, therefore the heart of the sons of men is fully set in them to do evil." *Eccl. 8:11*

I. MANY SIN BECAUSE THEY THINK THEY ARE "GETTING AWAY WITH IT."
  1. "Be sure your sin will find you out."
  2. "Whatsoever a man soweth, that shall he also reap."

II. GOD DELAYS HIS JUDGEMENTS AS AN ACT OF MERCY, TO GIVE TIME FOR REPENTANCE.
  1. "While the lamp holds out to burn,
     The vilest sinner may return."
     —Isaac Watts
  2. Eventually, the tares will be gathered and burned, while the good wheat will be garnered.

III. THE JUDGMENT IS INEVITABLE AND INESCAPABLE.
  1. "We must all appear before the judgment seat of Christ." No exceptions.
  2. "After a long time the lord of those servants cometh, and reckoneth with them."

111. LIFE AT ITS BEST

"Whatsoever thy hand findeth to do, do it with thy might." *Eccl. 9:10*

Well has it been said: "A task worth doing, and friends worth having, make life worth living."

I. "A TASK WORTH DOING"
  1. The work of the church and the Kingdom
  2. Labor of love
  3. Worthy of all we have or are
  4. "Too many petty causes get too much loyalty."

II. "FRIENDS WORTH HAVING"
  1. No friends like Christian friends
  2. "Blest be the tie that binds."

III. "MAKE LIFE WORTH LIVING"
  1. Longfellow's "Village Blacksmith." Had confidence of his neighbors; sat on Sunday in the church; his labors were worth while; at night he had "earned a night's repose."
  2. Christians at their best live life at its best.

112. ISAIAH'S VISION

"In the year that king Uzziah died I saw also the Lord sitting upon a throne, high and lifted up, and his train filled the temple." *Isa. 6:1*

I. ISAIAH LOOKED UP.
  1. "I saw . . . the Lord . . . , high and lifted up."
  2. Church worship gives us visions of God.

II. ISAIAH LOOKED WITHIN.
  1. "Woe is me!"
  2. What we see when we look within may distress us.

III. ISAIAH LOOKED ABOUT.
  1. Saw the need; heard the challenge to serve.
  2. "Here am I; send me."

113. THE ANTIDOTE TO FEAR

"Fear thou not; for I am with thee: be not dismayed; for I am thy God: I will strengthen thee; I will help thee; yea, I will uphold thee with the right hand of my righteousness." *Isa. 41:10*

The text offers three reasons why the Christian should not be fearful:

I. GOD'S PRESENCE
   1. "I am with thee." Powerful, wise, loving.
   2. "He leadeth me."
II. GOD'S RELATIONSHIP
   1. "I am *thy* God." Guardianship; blessing.
   2. We can trust "our Father."
III. GOD'S PROMISE
   1. "I will strengthen thee."
   2. "I will help thee."
   3. "I will uphold thee."

—*Seeds and Saplings*

114. LOOK!

"Look, ye blind, that ye may see." *Isa. 42:18*

I. LOOK BACK.
(Remember God's goodness, your sins.)
II. LOOK UP.
(In praise: "Bless the Lord, O my soul.")
III. LOOK DOWN.
(In humility: "Let him that thinketh he standeth take heed lest he fall.")
IV. LOOK FORWARD.
(With confidence)
V. LOOK WITHIN.
(Daily, thoroughly)
VI. LOOK AROUND.
(Be vigilant.)
VII. LOOK UNTO JESUS.
("The author and finisher of our faith")

—J. W. Mills

115. THE HABITATIONS OF GOD

"Thus saith the high and lofty One that inhabiteth eternity, whose name is Holy; I dwell in the high and holy place, with him also that is of a contrite and humble spirit, to revive the spirit of the humble, and to revive the heart of the contrite ones." *Isa. 57:15*

I. GOD INHABITS INFINITE TIME.
   1. "I change not."
   2. "Same yesterday, and to day, and for ever"
   3. God fills immeasurable time to its utmost dimension, every moment of eternity, past, present, and to be.
II. GOD INHABITS INFINITE SPACE.
   1. Ps. 139:7-10
   2. Acts 17:24-28
III. GOD INHABITS SELECTED SPACE.
   1. "The Lord is in his holy temple."
   2. In the hearts of those who open the door to him (Rev. 3:20)
   3. Text: "with him also that is of a contrite and humble spirit."

116. THE LORD OUR GUIDE

"The Lord shall guide thee continually." *Isa. 58:11*

I. WHY WE NEED A GUIDE
   1. We are ignorant of the way.
   2. We so easily stray from the right pathway.
II. WHY GOD IS THE BEST GUIDE
   1. He knows the way.
   2. He knows the trials and hardships we shall face.
   3. He knows the perils.
   4. He is our Father, and as such he will be kind and considerate.
III. REASONS WHY WE SHOULD FOLLOW HIM NOW
   1. "No time like the present."
   2. Tomorrow may never come.
   3. Better play safe.
   4. The sooner we accept his guidance, the sooner our joy and peace are assured.

117. THE LIGHT OF THE GOSPEL

"Arise, shine; for thy light is come, and the glory of the Lord is risen upon thee." *Isa. 60:1*

The effect of the light is to make the darkness more acute, by contrast:

I. THE ENLIGHTENMENT OF FAITH
   1. Compare with the boasted enlightenment of reason.
   2. The world's cleverness does not lead to truth.

II. THE ENLIGHTENMENT OF NATIONS THAT HAVE RECEIVED THE TRUTH
   1. Compare with surrounding heathenism.
   2. "Before and after"

III. THE ENLIGHTENMENT OF INDIVIDUALS WHO HAVE RECEIVED THE TRUTH
   1. Compare with those who remain in sin.
   2. "Whereas I was blind, now I see."

Application:

It is the Christian's duty to seek more and more light.

It is the Church's duty to "send the light."

118. HIS LOVINGKINDNESS

"I will mention the lovingkindnesses of the Lord." *Isa. 63:7*

1. It is marvelous (Ps. 17:7).
2. It is better than life (Ps. 63:3).
3. We are drawn by it (Jer. 31:3).
4. We are quickened by it (Ps. 119:88).
5. We are crowned with it (Ps. 103:4).
6. We should think of it (Ps. 48:9).
7. We should sing praise of it (Ps. 138:1-2).
8. We should speak of it. (Isa. 63:7).

119. GADDING ABOUT

"Why gaddest thou about so much?" *Jer. 2:36*

Gad was the seventh son of Jacob and head of one of the tribes of Israel. The tribe was nomadic, restless, lacking in stability. The term "gadding" seems to have originated from the transient habits of the tribe of Gad.

There are many modern "gadabouts," and they are not confined to Jewry.

I. DOMESTIC GADABOUTS
   1. Many, dissatisfied with home life, go far and wide in search of pleasure.
   2. Many broken homes result.

II. GADABOUTS IN THE REALM OF EMPLOYMENT
   1. Some do not stick to one job very long, are always looking for "greener pastures."
   2. "Looking for a soft job is a job for a soft man."
   3. Readjustments necessary at times, but with many they are just habit; natural discontent.

III. RELIGIOUS GADABOUTS
   1. Interchurch fellowship and visitation are much in order, but many just "shop around."
   2. There are many "church tramps."
   3. Even preachers have become gadabouts.

120. OLD PATHS

"Thus saith the Lord, Stand ye in the ways, and see, and ask for the old paths, where is the good way, and walk therein, and ye shall find rest for your souls." *Jer. 6:16*

The old path

I. IS A MOUNTAIN PATH.
   1. "Who shall *ascend* into the hill of the Lord?"
   2. It is not ease, but effort; not facility, but difficulty, that brings out the nobler qualities of the soul.

II. IS A THORNY PATH.
   1. Paul found it so. Thorn in the flesh.
   2. Jesus warned his disciples of the dangers and hardships ahead.

III. IT IS A BLOOD-MARKED PATH.
1. The Via Dolorosa, the Way of the Cross
2. Early adventurers blazed trails in the wilderness with axes; Jesus blazed the pathway to heaven with his own precious blood.

IV. IS STRAIGHT AND NARROW.
1. Not easy to walk on
2. One has to "watch his step."

V. LEADS TO GOD.

---

121. AS GOOD AS GOLD

"The precious sons of Zion, comparable to fine gold. . . ."
Lam. 4:2

1. In its natural state of little use
2. In the refiner's hands, dross removed
3. In the craftsman's hands, fashioned and polished
4. Grows dim through contact with the world's defilements
5. Loses luster when not in use

---

122. HOW IS YOUR SIGHT?

"Son of man, thou dwellest in the midst of a rebellious house, which have eyes to see, and see not; they have ears to hear, and hear not." *Ezek. 12:2*

Matthew Henry: "There are none so blind as those who will not see."

I. MANY ARE BLIND TO THE TREASURES OF THE BIBLE.
1. Illustration: A young man inherited a family Bible, but he never opened it. He lived in poverty. In his old age he discovered his parents had placed among its pages much money—bills of large denominations.
2. The Bible is a mine of precious treasure.
3. Psalmist: "Open thou mine eyes, that I may behold wondrous things out of thy law."

II. MANY SEE NOTHING IN THE CHURCH OR IN CHURCH SUPPORT.
1. Absence from worship indicates their evaluation of the church.
2. Failure to give financial support is another indication that some "see not."

III. SOME SEE NOTHING IN EVANGELISM.

IV. SOME SEE NOTHING IN MISSIONARY WORK.

V. SOME SEE NOTHING IN THE CROSS OF CHRIST.
1. Crucifiers of Jesus: "Sitting down they watched him there." But they saw nothing significant.
2. "Is it nothing to you, all ye that pass by?"

Application: How well do you see?

---

123. A LIBEL AGAINST GOD

"As I live, saith the Lord God, I have no pleasure in the death of the wicked." *Ezek. 33:11*

Many have taught that God has found a certain amount of satisfaction in taking vengeance upon the sinner. This is manifestly untrue.

God has no pleasure in the punishment of the wicked.

I. THIS IS POSITIVELY AFFIRMED IN THE TEXT.
1. "As I live, saith the Lord." A solemn oath.
2. "The Lord is . . . not willing that any should perish."

II. THE CHARACTER OF GOD SUBSTANTIATES THIS.
1. "God is love."
2. God is our Father.

III. GOD HAS PROVED IT BY SENDING HIS SON TO REDEEM SINNERS AND OBVIATE THEIR PUNISHMENT.

124. SHOWERS OF BLESSING

"There shall be showers of blessing." *Ezek. 34:26*

The word "blessing" is one which belongs strictly to the vocabulary of religion. Irreligious people do not make much use of the word, and properly so.

God promises his own "showers of blessing."

I. COPIOUS BLESSINGS
   1. "Showers," not just a few drops, or sprinkling.
   2. "Count your many blessings. . . . It will surprise you. . . ."

II. THE TIMELINESS OF THE BLESSINGS
   1. "In his season"
   2. God does all things well. Our times are in his hands.

III. THE DIFFUSION OF HIS BLESSINGS
   1. "The places round about"
   2. "On the just and on the unjust." The wicked receive blessings because of the proximity of the righteous.

125. DRY BONES

"He said unto me, Son of man, can these bones live?" *Ezek. 37:3*

Ezekiel's vision has obvious implications:

I. "DRY BONES" ALL ABOUT US
   1. Many people seem utterly hopeless insofar as spiritual life is concerned.
   2. In the old revival-meeting days such people were referred to as "gospel hardened."

II. WITH GOD'S HELP, NO CASE IS HOPELESS
   1. The bones Ezekiel saw were dry, "very dry."
   2. Many poor prospects have become converts to Christianity: Saul of Tarsus, the demoniac of Gadara, Zacchaeus, Mary Magdalene.
   3. God "is able . . . to save . . . to the uttermost."
   4. "You hath he quickened, who were dead in trespasses and sins." Paul.

III. THE PROCEDURE
   1. "Prophesy . . . unto them, . . . and say, . . .
   2. Ezekiel did as instructed (verse 7). Results.
   3. Jesus said: "The words that I speak . . . , they are spirit, and they are life."
   4. God's Word, faithfully taught, preached, lived, brings to life many who were dead in sin.

126. HE IS ABLE

"Our God whom we serve is able to deliver us." *Dan. 3:17*

He is able:

1. To save to the uttermost (Heb. 7:25).

2. To make all grace abound (II Cor. 9:8).

3. To succor the tempted (Heb. 2:18).

4. To make us stand (Rom. 14:4).

5. To keep us from falling (Jude 24).

6. To subdue all things (Phil. 3:21).

7. To keep that committed to him (II Tim. 1:12).

8. To perform what he has promised (Rom. 4:21).

9. To do above all we ask or think (Eph. 3:20).

—F. S. Shepard

127. BACKSLIDING

"Come, and let us return unto the Lord: for he hath torn, and he will heal us; he hath smitten, and he will bind us up." *Hos. 6:1*

Backsliding is:

1. Turning from God (I Kings 11:9).

2. Leaving the first love (Rev. 2:4).

3. Departing from the teachings of the gospel (II Cor. 11:3; Gal. 3:1-3; 5:4, 7).

4. Displeasing to God (Ps. 78: 57, 59).

5. Pardonable (II Chron. 7:14; Jer. 3:12; 31:20; 36:3).

128. WHAT TIME IS IT?

"It is time to seek the Lord."
Hos. 10:12

I. IT IS TIME TO SEEK THE LORD
(A call to the sinner)

II. IT IS HIGH TIME TO AWAKE OUT OF SLEEP. (Rom. 13: 12)
(A warning to the saint)

III. "IT IS TIME FOR THEE, LORD, TO WORK." (Ps. 119:126)
(A prayer to the Lord)

—Charles Edwards

129. WRONG-WAY JONAH

"But Jonah rose up to flee unto Tarshish from the presence of the Lord." *Jon. 1:3*

God ordered Jonah to duty at Nineveh. He fled in the opposite direction. Why did Jonah try to sidestep responsibility?

I. HE MAY HAVE FELT UNEQUAL TO THE TASK.
1. It was quite "a big order."
2. Many of us would quake at such an assignment.

II. HE MAY HAVE FELT HE HAD BEEN DOING ENOUGH FOR GOD'S CAUSE.
1. Many today feel they are overworked by the church.
2. The attitude of many: "Let George do it."

III. JONAH MAY HAVE FELT THE TASK WAS TOO UNPLEASANT
1. An unpopular thing to tell people of their sins
2. An unpopular thing to warn of doom
3. John the Baptist beheaded because he dared to accuse Herod of wrongdoing

IV. PERHAPS JONAH HONESTLY FELT HE DID NOT HAVE THE TIME, TALENT, RESOURCES, ESSENTIAL TO THE JOB.
1. Such, at least, are the excuses of many today.
2. "Never say 'No' to God."

V. BUT JONAH CAME TO HIMSELF AND DID HIS JOB.

130. REVIVE US AGAIN!

"O Lord, revive thy work."
Hab. 3:2

The Church needs:

I. A GREAT DOWN-POURING
1. Revivals are not "gotten up," but down from above.
2. The promise of the Holy Spirit

II. A GREAT UP-RISING
1. "Awake thou that sleepest."
2. Ezekiel's vision of the valley of dry bones

III. A GREAT OUT-REACHING
1. Jerusalem, Judea, Samaria, the uttermost parts of the earth
2. "Your love has a broken pinion if it cannot fly across the ocean."

IV. A GREAT IN-GATHERING
1. "Go out . . . , and compel them to come in."
2. The army of the Lord needs recruits, replacements.

- failure
- frustration
- fretfulness

II
New Testament Texts

131. GOD WITH US

"They shall call his name Emmanuel, which being interpreted is, God with us." *Matt. 1:23*

Jesus is God with us in:
1. Human form
2. Divine sympathy
3. Redeeming love
4. Heavenly glory

—*Expositor's Dictionary of Texts*

132. WHERE IS HE?

"Where is he that is born King of the Jews?" *Matt. 2:2a*

I. "Where Is He?"
   1. Such was the Magi's inquiry.
   2. Job: "Oh that I knew where I might find him!"
   3. The quest of the ages is the quest for God.

II. Where Has God Been Found?
   1. In nature: "The heavens declare the glory of God; and the firmament sheweth his handywork."
   2. In scripture: "They are they which testify of me."
   3. In the temple: "The Lord is in his holy temple." "Where two or three are gathered. . . ."
   4. In paths of service: "Inasmuch as ye have done it unto one of the least . . . ye have done it unto me."

III. "Where Is He?"
   1. The best answer: He is in the hearts of those who allow him to come in.
   2. "If any man . . . [will] open the door, I will come in to him."

Application: Does the world see Jesus in you?

133. THE MAGI

"We have seen his star in the east, and are come to worship him." *Matt. 2:2*

I. True Wisdom
   1. It is good evidence of superior intelligence in men to seek Christ.
   2. The great intellectuals of the ages accept his sovereignty.

II. Little Knowledge
   1. The Magi had very little information to help them, but they made good use of what they had.
   2. Used what light they had.

III. Much Faith
   1. Theirs was an adventure of faith, and God did not disappoint them.
   2. "Seek, and ye shall find."

IV. Sincere Worship
   1. "Fell down [bowed low], and worshipped him."
   2. Not affectation, pageantry, dramatics. It was in spirit and in truth.

V. Spirit Led
   1. "Being warned of God . . . , they departed . . . another way."
   2. "He will guide you into all truth."

134. THE MESSAGE OF JOHN THE BAPTIST

"In those days came John the Baptist, preaching in the wilderness of Judaea." *Matt. 3:1*

I. He Preached Repentance. Matt. 3:2.
   (Later, Jesus began his preaching with the same text.)

II. He Preached Christ
   ("Behold the Lamb of God, which taketh away the sin of the world." John 1:29.)

III. He Preached a Practical Religion.
   ("Bring forth . . . fruits." Matt. 3:8.)

IV. He Bore Witness to the Office and Work of the Holy Spirit.
   (Matt. 3:11.)

V. He Preached Salvation for the Penitent and Punishment for the Impenitent. (Matt. 3:12.)

Application: The eulogy of Jesus on John. Matt. 11:11.

135. FOLLOW ME

"He saith unto them, Follow me, and I will make you fishers of men."
Matt. 4:19

I. Whom?
  1. Not simply a human teacher, but Jesus, who qualified himself by his earthly life, with his temptations, toils, sufferings, to be the true Leader of men.
  2. "A teacher come from God."

II. How?
  1. We cannot follow his person, as the disciples did when upon earth.
  2. But we may obey his teachings.
  3. And we may copy his example.

III. Why?
  1. There is no leader equal to Christ.
  2. If we follow him, we shall be in good company.
  3. Only thus can we escape spiritual danger and eternal death.

IV. Whither?
  1. To God
  2. To heaven

V. When?
  1. Now: "Now is the accepted time."
  2. Always: "Even unto the end. . . ."

—F. J. Austin

136. FOLLOWING CHRIST

"And they straightway left their nets, and followed him."
Matt. 4:20

F—Forsaking the old life (II Cor. 5:17).
O—Obeying the Lord's word (John 21:22).
L—Looking not behind (Luke 9:62).
L—Looking unto Jesus (Heb. 12:2).
O—Onward to the end (Phil. 3:13-14).
W—Watching unto prayer (Mark 13:33).

137. THE GREAT TEACHER

"And he opened his mouth, and taught them." *Matt. 5:2*

An analysis of the teaching methods and skills of Jesus can give us some excellent suggestions as to our own techniques.

I. He Knew His Bible. (Only the Old Testament in existence then.)
  1. His teachings saturated with quotations from O. T.
  2. Always ready to quote appropriate passages: his temptation by the devil in the wilderness
  3. Used Septuagint (the revised version of that day).

II. Unconventional as to Time or Place
  1. Didn't have to have a classroom and equipment.
  2. Reminds of an old definition of a university: "Mark Hopkins on one end of a log, and a farm boy on the other end."

III. He Preferred the Few, Rather Than Multitudes.
  1. His greatest utterances were to individuals, or small groups.
  2. Nicodemus; the woman of Samaria; disciples

IV. His Teaching Was Practical, Down to Earth.
  1. Jesus came to grips with everyday problems.
  2. Used terms and illustrations the people could understand. "Common people heard him gladly."

V. HIS TEACHING WAS PURPOSEFUL.
   1. He taught "for a verdict."
   2. He went to the very heart of a problem.

VI. HE TAUGHT BY HIS LIFE.
   1. "The life was the light of men."
   2. "What you are rings so loudly in my ears, I cannot hear you say what you are." (Emerson.)

---

138. THE SALT OF THE EARTH

"Ye are the salt of the earth: but if the salt have lost his savour, wherewith shall it be salted?" *Matt. 5:13*

Christians should be:

1. An appetizing influence
2. A purifying influence
3. A preservative influence

---

139. THREE MARKS OF THE CHRISTIAN

"Ye are the salt of the earth. . . . Ye are the light of the world. A city that is set on an hill cannot be hid." *Matt. 5:13-14*

I. THE SALT OF THE EARTH
   1. It preserves.
   2. It seasons.
   3. It freshens.

II. THE LIGHT OF THE WORLD
   1. It gives light.
   2. It enlightens.
   3. It exposes evil.

III. A CITY SET ON A HILL
   1. It is seen by all.
   2. It is a landmark, a guide.
   3. It cannot be moved.

—V. E. R.

---

140. A BRIEF SERMON

"Ye are the light of the world." *Matt. 5:14*

Theme: "A city that is set on an hill cannot be hid. Neither do men light a candle, and put it under a bushel, but on a candlestick; and it giveth light unto all that are in the house."

Exhortation: "Let your light so shine before men, that they may see your good works, and glorify your Father which is in heaven."

—Edwin Hamlin Carr

---

141. DEFECTIVE RELIGION

"Except your righteousness shall exceed the righteousness of the scribes and Pharisees, ye shall in no case enter into the kingdom of heaven." *Matt. 5:20*

The religion of the scribes and Pharisees was defective. It was:

I. ALL ON THE SURFACE
   1. "Whited sepulchres"
   2. "To be seen of men"

II. OF THE HEAD AND NOT OF THE HEART
   1. "This people honoureth me with their lips, but their heart is far from me."
   2. Mechanical religion

III. ARISTOCRATIC AND EXCLUSIVE
   1. The Pharisee and publican at prayer
   2. Egotistical

IV. CONCERNED WITH THE LETTER OF THE LAW, WHILE IGNORING THE SPIRIT OF IT

V. HYPOCRITICAL AND INSINCERE
   1. "Devour widows' houses"
   2. Paid Jesus compliments while planning his death.

VI. WE HAVE TO EXCEED THIS.

---

142. FIRST THINGS FIRST

"Seek ye first the kingdom of God, . . . and all these things shall be added unto you." *Matt. 6:33*

1. Seek ye first the *kingdom of God.*

2. *Seek* ye first the kingdom of God.

3. Seek *ye* first the kingdom of God.

4. Seek ye *first* the kingdom of God.

5. And *all* these things shall be added unto you.

—M. R. Drury

143. FACTORS IN PRAYER

"Ask, and it shall be given you; seek, and ye shall find; knock, and it shall be opened unto you."

Matt. 7:7

I. The Simplicity of Prayer
   1. "Ask" (verse 7*a*).
   2. Asking gets the response of a gift (verse 8*a*)

II. The Intensity of Prayer
   1. "Seek" (verse 7*b*).
   2. Seeking gets the response of a discovery (verse 8*b;* Jer. 29:13).

III. The Persistency of Prayer
   1. "Knock" (verse 7*c*).
   2. Knocking gets the response of an entrance into the secret treasures of divine resources (verse 8*c;* Isa. 45:1-3).

—Ezra S. Gerig

144. THE GOLDEN RULE

"Therefore all things whatsoever ye would that men should do to you, do ye even so to them."

Matt. 7:12

The Golden Rule is:

1. Golden—sound through and through
2. Brief—easy to understand and easy to remember
3. Comprehensive—"all things whatsoever"
4. Reasonable—based on justice, equality
5. Beneficent—in relation to ourselves and to others
6. An ideal principle—some say it should be called the "Golden Principle," because principles do not change and rules do.

145. THE HEM OF CHRIST'S GARMENT

"And, behold, a woman . . . came behind him, and touched the hem of his garment." *Matt. 9:20*

The hem of Christ's garment can still be touched. For what is this hem but that through which blessing passed from him to others?

There are many things whereby the virtue and blessings of Christ may be appropriated by men.

I. Some Find the "Hem of Christ's Garment" in Nature
   ("Nature," says Goethe, "is the visible garment of God, wrought by God's fingers on time's roaring loom.")

II. Some See in Art the "Hem of Christ's Garment."
   (The world's religious masterpieces of paintings, sculpture, architecture, music, literature.)

III. The Holy Bible Is a "Hem of Christ's Garment."
   (Multitudes have come into contact with it to their joy and happiness; imparting strength and healing.)

IV. The Ministries of the Church May Be "the Hem of Christ's Garment" to Some.

V. The Sacrament of the Lord's Supper Channels the Virtue of Christ into the Lives of Men.

—Adapted from W. M. Clow, *The Cross in Christian Experience*

146. THE LORD OF LIFE IN THE CHAMBER OF DEATH

"When the people were put forth, he went in, and took her by the hand, and the maid arose."

Matt. 9:25

I. His Mercy in Going
   (A ruler's house)

II. His Forbearance
   (No unkind word to those who laughed)

III. His Compassion for the Parents

"[She] sleepeth."

IV. HIS TENDERNESS TO THE CHILD
("Took her by the hand")

V. HIS POWER OVER DEATH
("The maid arose.")

VI. HIS THOUGHTFUL CARE
("Commanded that something should be given her to eat." Mark 5:43.)

—*Homiletic Commentary*

147. THE GOSPEL AND THE POOR

"The poor have the gospel preached to them." *Matt. 11:5*

The Gospel is:

I. PLAIN
(The uneducated can understand it.)

II. SYMPATHETIC
(The lowly can appreciate it.)

III. ELEVATING
(The humble are raised by it.)

IV. COMPENSATING
(The destitute are enriched by it.)

—*Biblical Encyclopedia*

148. THE EASY YOKE AND THE LIGHT BURDEN

"My yoke is easy, and my burden is light." *Matt. 11:30*

The yoke of Christ is easy, and his burden is light, because:

1. It is borne with an approving conscience.
2. It is borne in love.
3. It is borne with the help of the Spirit of God.
4. It becomes lighter the longer it is borne.
5. We are sustained by the blessed hope of heaven and endless happiness.

—W. M. Taylor

149. THE WORTH OF A MAN

"How much . . . is a man better than a sheep?" *Matt. 12:12*

The soul of man is immortal. Then three things follow:

1. One man is worth just as much as another. Manhood is not measured by the purse, nor by inches, nor by brains.
2. We ought to be more concerned about the salvation of a man than the safety of a sheep. That goes without saying—but it also goes without practicing.
3. We ought to be more concerned about our own souls than some of us are.

—W. E. Biederwolf

150. TELLING JESUS

"His disciples . . . went and told Jesus." *Matt. 14:12*

Following the tragic death of their leader, John the Baptist, his friends "came, and took up the body, and buried it, and went and told Jesus."

What they did was a natural thing for them to do, and millions have done likewise. There are good reasons for going to Jesus with our sorrows, burdens, and problems.

I. HE IS OUR BEST FRIEND.
1. "Sticketh closer than a brother."
2. "What a Friend we have in Jesus!"

II. HE IS COMPASSIONATE
1. He enters sympathetically into our joys and sorrows.
2. Jesus wept at Lazarus' tomb.

III. HE IS UNDERSTANDING.

IV. HE HAS THE WORDS OF ETERNAL LIFE.

151. THE COMPASSION OF JESUS

"Jesus went forth, and saw a great multitude, and was moved with compassion toward them." *Matt. 14:14*

I. JESUS "SAW A GREAT MULTITUDE."
1. He looked upon them, informed himself.
2. He didn't turn his head away.

3. He didn't do as did the priest and Levite en route to Jericho.
4. Jesus urged: "Lift up your eyes, and look. . . ."

II. JESUS "WAS MOVED WITH COMPASSION."
1. He was sorry for the hungry, the sick, the downtrodden, the sinful.
2. Jesus cares.
3. "He hath borne our griefs, and carried our sorrows."

III. JESUS DID SOMETHING ABOUT THESE NEEDS.
1. He ordered his followers: "Give ye them to eat."
2. He surveyed resources.
3. Systematic distribution of food
4. He practiced rigid economy. "Gather up the fragments."

152. THE DEITY OF CHRIST

"Thou art the Christ, the Son of the living God." *Matt. 16:16*

That Christ is divine is:

1. Proclaimed by the Father (Matt. 1:23; John 1:1).

2. Claimed by the Son (John 5:21; 10:30; Rev. 1:8).

3. Witnessed by the Spirit. (Heb. 1:8; I Pet. 3:15).

4. Acclaimed by disciples (Matt. 16:16; John 20:28).

5. Acknowledged by angels (Heb. 1:6; Rev. 5:11-12.)

6. Conceded by demons (Mark 5:7; Jas. 2:19; Luke 8:28).

7. Manifested by his works (Luke 7:21; John 5:36).

153. THE CHURCH ON THE ROCK

"Upon this rock I will build my church; and the gates of hell shall not prevail against it." *Matt. 16:18*

I. THE NATURE OF THE CHRISTIAN CHURCH
1. Composed of true believers in Christ, who have accepted him as their personal Saviour and Lord, and have professed their faith in public
2. There's a real difference between a church and a church building.

II. THE OWNER OF THE CHRISTIAN CHURCH
1. Jesus said: "my church."
2. Probably correct to associate human founders and benefactors with denominations and local churches, but do not forget it is Christ's Church.
3. His by costly purchase
4. His by divine oversight and providential care

III. THE FOUNDATION OF THE CHRISTIAN CHURCH—"THIS ROCK"
1. Safety
2. Elevation
3. Strength
4. Permanence

IV. THE SAFETY OF THE CHRISTIAN CHURCH
1. Powers of darkness and evil shall not prevail against it.
2. Time and natural forces of disintegration will have no adverse effect upon it.
3. Militant on earth; triumphant in heaven

154. THE PRESENCE

"Where two or three are gathered together in my name, there am I in the midst of them." *Matt. 18:20*

1. Numbers are not requisite to worship.

2. The mystical presence is very real to those with spiritual insight.

3. Where the Spirit of Christ is, there Christ is.

4. Personal fellowship with

Christ is the heart and hope of his Church.

—Walter D. Mehrling

155. IDOLATRY VS. IDLETRY

"Why stand ye here all the day idle?" *Matt. 20:6*

"Idletry" may not be in the dictionary, but there is a great deal of it in the church. Many who would resent being called idolators certainly must admit to being "idletors."

If you are an idle Christian, it isn't because:

I. THERE IS NOTHING TO DO.
   1. "The harvest truly is plenteous."
   2. "The duty of the many should not be the task of a few."

II. THERE IS PLENTY OF TIME.
   1. Time is running out on us.
   2. There is much to be done and little time in which to to do it.
   3. "I must work . . . , while it is day."

III. THE PAY IS SMALL.
   1. Godliness is profitable, here and hereafter.
   2. "Behold, I come quickly; and my reward is with me."

Application: "Woe to them that are at ease in Zion."

156. USEFUL VS. ORNAMENTAL CHRISTIANS

"When he saw a fig tree in the way, he came to it, and found nothing thereon, but leaves only, and said unto it, Let no fruit grow on thee henceforward for ever. And presently the fig tree withered away." *Matt. 21:19*

I. THIS MIRACLE IS A SYMBOLICAL ACT.
   1. Dramatizes sin of unfruitfulness
   2. Rebuke of sham, hypocrisy, false appearances
   3. "*Esse quam videri.*" ("To be rather than to seem")

II. THE MIRACLE POINTS UP THE FACT THAT CHRIST DEMANDS FRUITS OF HIS FOLLOWERS.
   1. Christians are to be useful as well as ornamental.
   2. "I have . . . ordained you, that ye should go and bring forth fruit."
   3. "Bring forth . . . fruits meet for repentance."
   4. James: "Faith without works is dead."
   5. Jesus: "By their fruits ye shall know them."

III. THE MIRACLE IS A SOLEMN WARNING.
   1. "Every tree which bringeth not forth . . . hewn down, and cast into the fire."
   2. Trees were taxed in Palestine; therefore destroyed if unfruitful.

IV. MANY ARE GUILTY OF "SINS OF OMISSION."
   1. Jesus had much to say in condemnation of those who failed to produce fruits.
   2. Parables that drive home this fact: virgins, talents, rich fool, rich young ruler, Dives, priest and Levite, judgment ("Inasmuch as ye did it not. . . .")

Application: Are we useful Christians, or just ornamental?

157. FRIVOLOUS RELIGION

"But they made light of it." *Matt. 22:5*

Many make light of:

1. The opportunities of salvation
2. The cost of the Cross
3. The sanctity of the Sabbath day
4. The inspiration and authority of scripture
5. The values of worship
6. The uncertainties of life
7. The commands and warnings of God

8. The value of the immortal soul

158. THE KINGDOM OF GOD

"This gospel of the kingdom shall be preached in all the world."
Matt. 24:14

I. The King Is Our Lord Jesus Christ.
II. The Seat of the Kingdom Is the Soul.
II. The Spirit of the Kingdom Is Wise, Beneficent, and Holy.
IV. The Growth of the Kingdom Is Unostentatious, Irresistible, Noiseless.
V. The Boundaries of the Kingdom Are the Ends of the Earth.

—J. Burns

159. ARE YOU READY?

"Be ye also ready: for in such an hour as ye think not the Son of man cometh." *Matt. 24:44*

1. Ready to answer (I Pet. 3:15).
2. Ready to preach (Rom. 1:15).
3. Ready to distribute (I Tim. 6:18).
4. Ready for every good work (Tit. 3:1).
5. Ready to die (Acts 21:13).
6. Ready to meet the Lord (Luke 12:36).
7. Ready to enter heaven (Matt. 25:10).

160. A LOT OF FOOLISHNESS

"The foolish said unto the wise, Give us of your oil; for our lamps are gone out." *Matt. 25:8*

It's a lot of foolishness:

1. To expect a just God to overlook unpreparedness
2. To depend upon borrowing religion for the emergency
3. To depend upon morality to get you into heaven
4. To think there is plenty of time to get ready

To think that there is something someone else can do for you

the fact that you are unprepared

161. GOD'S MINUTE MEN

"Watch and pray, that ye enter not into temptation."
Matt. 26:41

The Christian should be ready at all times:

1. To defend his faith (I Pet. 3:15)
2. To bear testimony (Rom 1:15)
3. With intelligent charity (Rom. 12:13)
4. To do good (Tit. 3:1)
5. To depart this life (II Tim. 4:5-8)
6. To meet the Lord (Matt. 25:13)

162. FICKLE DISCIPLESHIP

"Then all the disciples forsook him, and fled." *Matt. 26:56*

I. Note When This Wholesale Desertion Took Place.
   1. Not on Palm Sunday. It was easy to be loyal when everything seemed to be going well. It is easy to be a soldier on parade.
   2. The desertion took place when Jesus needed friendship and loyalty most.

II. Why Did the Disciples Desert Jesus?
   1. They were wretchedly tired. The long trek from Galilee; the excitement in Jerusalem; little rest for many days.
   2. Their vision of empire was blasted. Jesus seemed impotent. They couldn't grasp the idea of a spiritual kingdom. No idea of a resurrection.
   3. They acted impulsively. A quick decision. They were caught off guard.
   4. They were afraid for their lives. What was happening to Jesus might happen to them.

III. WHY DO MODERN DISCIPLES DESERT JESUS?
1. Many do so for lesser reasons than the early disciples.
2. Worldliness; laziness; selfishness; lack of love for Christ and the Church

163. PONTIUS PILATE

"[Pilate] took water, and washed his hands before the multitude, saying, I am innocent of the blood of this just person."
Matt. 27:24

1. The story of Pilate shows a man can really deceive himself, for a time.
2. Pilate has many counterparts in the modern world, people afraid to take a stand for the right; afraid to take a stand on moral issues.
3. Evading responsibility is a despicable business. For such we have only contempt.
4. Pilate thought Jesus was on trial before him, but the reverse was true.
5. The tradition of Pilate's sad end. Died insane, trying to wash Jesus' blood from his hands.
6. Question: What will you do with Jesus?

164. LOOKING BUT NOT SEEING

"And sitting down they watched him there." *Matt. 27:36*

The soldiers who nailed Jesus to the cross were doing their routine work. They saw nothing significant in what was taking place. They nonchalantly watched.

What should *we* see in the cross?

I. A SYMBOL OF THE AWFULNESS OF SIN
1. How terrible a thing sin must be if God would go to such lengths to provide an antidote!
2. "Sin, when it is finished, bringeth forth death."

II. A SYMBOL OF "LOVE DIVINE, ALL LOVES EXCELLING"
1. "Greater love hath no man than this."
2. "Two wonders I confess:
The wonders of redeeming love
And my unworthiness."

III. THE CENTRAL SYMBOL OF THE CHRISTIAN'S FAITH
1. The signpost that points the pilgrim to heaven
2. "I must needs go home by the way of the cross."
3. "All the light of sacred story
Gathers round its head sublime."

165. HOLD UP YOUR CORNER

"They come unto him, bringing one sick of the palsy, which was borne of four." *Mark 2:3*

I. JESUS IS "THE GREAT PHYSICIAN."
1. Interested in both the souls and bodies of men
2. It is the duty of the Church to bring the sin-sick to Christ.

II. IT TAKES CO-OPERATION TO BRING FOLKS TO CHRIST.
1. "Borne of four"
2. Suppose one man had let go his corner!
3. Pastors can be at but one corner; laymen needed.

III. THE MANNER IN WHICH THESE FRIENDS HELD UP THEIR CORNERS.
1. Cheerfully, we assume; it couldn't have been otherwise. It was a labor of love, and love always wears a smile.
2. Steadily. Kept step. That made it easier for all. Soul winning and church work move more smoothly when all keep in step.
3. Perseveringly. Undaunted by obstacles, they literally "raised the roof" to accomplish their purpose.

If we do our part — Jesus will do the rest
opposition
eyes — didn't stop Jesus — Glory
"we never saw it on this fashion"

4. Prayerfully. They interceded with Jesus to heal their friend.

Application: In the great work of bringing the sin-sick to Christ, are you holding up your corner?

✓

166. THE IMPATIENCE OF JESUS

"And . . . he . . . looked around about on them with anger."
Mark 3:5

We place so much emphasis upon the gentleness, meekness, compassion, and forgiveness of Christ that we may overlook the sterner aspects of his nature.

I. Jesus Had No Patience with Sin in Any of Its Manifestations.
1. Loved sinners, but hated the sin that despoiled their lives
2. Often found it necessary to be militant in dealing with sin and wilful sinners

II. Instances of His Impatience with Sin and Sinful Attitudes
1. Impatient with Pharisees who would rather a man remain in suffering than be healed on the Sabbath
2. Denounced scribes and Pharisees for hypocrisy
3. Rebuked those who would prevent children from coming to him
4. Impatient with those who condemned the woman taken in a social sin, who were themselves as guilty as she
5. Impatient with those who turned the house of prayer into a market place
6. Impatient with Dives; also the rich fool
7. Impatient with those who wanted an easy way into the Kingdom

167. HEROD CELEBRATES HIS BIRTHDAY

"Herod on his birthday made a supper to his lords." *Mark 6:21*

Observations on the celebration:

I. The Depravity of Human Nature
1. Herod
2. Herodias
3. Herodias' daughter

II. Revelry Leads to Rashness.
1. Conspiracy
2. Murder

III. Many Make Crime out of Sport.

IV. Many Innocent People Suffer as a Consequence of the Wild Parties of Others.

V. It Is Foolish to Keep a Foolish Promise.

168. SHARING THE GOSPEL

"Give ye them to eat."
Mark 6:37

I. The World Needs What Christ Has to Offer.

II. The Bread of Heaven Is in Unlimited Supply.

III. God Expects Us to Live Shared Lives.

IV. The More Love We Give to Others, the More We Shall Have for Ourselves.

169. HIDING JESUS

"He could not be hid."
Mark 7:24

I. Jesus Could Not Be Hid.
1. Wherever he went, his presence was discovered.
2. Multitudes followed.
3. Today, if Christ is around, his presence is soon felt.

II. He Would Not Be Hid.
1. While on earth in the flesh he had to seek obscurity on several occasions for needed rest; protection from enemies.
2. Yet he taught the necessity of his being "lifted up."
3. He wanted his followers to so live that he could be seen in them.

4. "Let your light . . . shine."

III. He Should Not Be Hid.
1. He is the panacea for all that ails the world.
2. "Christ is the answer."
3. Gratitude for our personal deliverance from sin should inspire us to share the gospel.

170. WHAT IT COSTS NOT TO BE A CHRISTIAN

"What shall it profit a man, if he shall gain the whole world, and lose his own soul?" *Mark 8:36*

Some place much emphasis upon the costs of discipleship to Christ, upon the demands of the Church. In fairness, we should contrast what it costs not to be a Christian.

I. The Sacrifice of Peace
1. "Thou wilt keep him in perfect peace, whose mind is stayed on thee."
2. "There is no peace, saith my God, to the wicked."

II. The Sacrifice of the Highest Joy
1. The non-Christian may have joy, but not the highest joy.
2. "That your joy may be full."

III. The Sacrifice of True Success in Life
1. One may make money, acquire fame, without being a Christian.
2. One may have all the world can offer, yet be a consummate failure.

IV. The Loss of One's Soul
1. "The wages of sin is death; but the gift of God is eternal life."
2. "The soul that sinneth, it shall die."

V. The Loss of Heaven
1. "Jesus saith unto him, I am the way, the truth, and the life: no man cometh unto the Father, but by me."
2. "Cast ye the unprofitable servant into outer darkness."

—Howard W. Pope

171. FAITH IN HONEST DOUBT

"Lord, I believe; help thou mine unbelief." *Mark 9:24*

Some species of doubt:

I. Doubts Arising from a Sinful Background

II. The Doubts of So-Called Skeptics—Who Think It Is Smart to Ridicule Religion

III. The Doubts of the Frustrated
1. Impatient for answers to prayer

IV. Honest Doubts
1. Even John the Baptist was guilty here.
2. Nicodemus: "How can these things be?"
3. Thomas: "Except I shall see . . . , I will not believe."
4. Text

Application: Get to really know Christ, and doubts will disappear. See II Tim. 1:12.

172. LIVES THAT LIFT

"Jesus took him by the hand, and lifted him up." *Mark 9:27*

In emulation of the Master, the disciples of Christ should strive to live lives that lift. What are some of the elements that go to make up such a life?

The life that lifts is:
1. A sympathetic life
2. A cheerful, hopeful life
3. A pure life
4. A spiritual life

173. THE MOTIVE SUPREME

"For my sake . . . ."
Mark 10:29

There are good, bad, and mixed motives behind Christian living and serving. The supreme motive is suggested in the text.

I. To Do Things for Christ's Sake Presumes Acquaintance with Christ.
1. It is improbable that we devote our lives to an unknown person.
2. If we know him, we will love him.
3. One thing to *know* Christ; another thing to *know about* him.

II. What This Supreme Motive Inspires
1. Obedience: "If ye love me, keep my commandments."
2. Cheerful service: "God loveth a cheerful giver" of time, talent, things."
3. Loyalty
4. Sacrifice: "I count all things but loss" (Paul).

Application: If it is for Jesus' sake we live the Christian way, it matters little whether appreciation and plaudits come from our fellow men.

174. CHRISTIAN FAITH

"And Jesus answering saith unto them, Have faith in God."
Mark 11:22

By faith
1. We live (Rom. 1:17).
2. We stand (II Cor. 1:24).
3. We walk (II Cor. 5:7).
4. We fight (I Tim. 6:12).
5. We overcome (I John 5:4).
6. We are justified (Rom. 3:28).
7. We have access to God's grace (Rom. 5:2).

—*The Preacher's Tool Basket*

175. CHRIST AND THE COMMON PEOPLE

"The common people heard him gladly." *Mark 12:37*

They heard him gladly because:

I. He Spoke with Sublime Simplicity.
1. He used words, terms, object lessons, within the grasp of all who heard.
2. He condemned theological arguments and "hairsplitting."
3. He put the spiritual food within their reach.

II. He Spoke with Tenderness, Sympathy, Compassion.
1. They knew he was their friend.
2. They saw his tears of compassion.

III. He Spoke of Heaven and Immortality.
1. "In my Father's house are many mansions."
2. "I am the resurrection, and the life."
3. "Thou hast the words of eternal life."

176. THE YOUTH OF JESUS

"Jesus increased in wisdom and stature, and in favour with God and man." *Luke 2:52*

The acts and attitudes of Jesus as a growing boy in Nazareth set an example for the young people of all time.

I. He Wrought with His Hands.
1. A carpenter
2. Grew up to abhor idleness

II. He Was a Student.
1. His textbooks: the Bible, nature, prayer, current events
2. A divinity student

III. He Was Obedient.
1. Subject unto his parents
2. Obeyed God
3. Yielded to civil authority

IV. He Lived Purposefully.
1. His one ambition was to be about his Father's business.
2. His temptation in the wilderness reveals his tenacity of purpose.

177. JESUS AND THE CHURCH

"As his custom was, he went into the synagogue on the sabbath day."
Luke 4:16

I. THE TEXT SUGGESTS THE DOMESTIC HABITS OF MARY AND JOSEPH.
   1. As much of a task to get their family off to the synagogue as for any modern family
   2. John Wesley was the fifteenth child of his mother, but he, with all the others, was brought up to keep the Sabbath holy.

II. THE TEXT SUGGESTS THE PERSONAL ATTITUDE OF JESUS TOWARD WORSHIP ON THE SABBATH.
   1. Having been trained "up in the way he should go," he needed no urging.
   2. Most of those who fill pews in the modern church were trained to do so from childhood.

III. JESUS MADE HIMSELF AVAILABLE TO HELP WITH THE SERVICE.
   1. Stood up to read. Offered to teach.
   2. Knew his Scriptures.

IV. THE HARSH TREATMENT ACCORDED HIM BY HIS FELLOW NAZARENES DIDN'T AFFECT HIS LOYALTY TO GOD.
   1. Literally thrown out of the synagogue. They even sought his life.
   2. Jesus exemplified his own teaching: "Blessed are ye, when men shall revile you, and persecute you."

178. AN ADVENTURE IN FAITH

"Master, we toiled all night, and took nothing: but at thy word I will let down the nets."

Luke 5:5 (*A.S.V.*)

Like other miracles, the miraculous draft of fishes had spiritual implications.

I. THE LORD'S WISDOM SHOULD NOT BE QUESTIONED.
   1. Peter hesitated, then acquiesced.
   2. Many of us question the wisdom of doing what the Lord tells us to do.

II. FAITH MUST NEVER DEMAND A RATIONAL BASIS.
   1. Reason can take us so far, but not all the way.
   2. We should do as the Lord instructs, even though we think it time and effort wasted.

III. THE CHURCH NEEDS TO "LAUNCH OUT INTO THE DEEP."
   1. We are too fearful to leave the shores.
   2. We are too content to fish in the shallows.
   3. "Attempt great things for God; expect great things from God."

IV. FAITH IS REWARDED, IF ACCOMPANIED BY DEEDS.
   1. "Faith without works is dead."
   2. "According to your faith be it unto you."

179. DIG DEEP

"Every one that cometh unto me, and heareth my words, and doeth them, I will show you to whom he is like: he is like a man building a house, who digged and went deep, and laid a foundation upon the rock." *Luke 6:47-48* (*A.S.V.*)

I. SOME BUILD WITHOUT A FOUNDATION.
   1. They live "on the surface."
   2. What they build, until the testing time comes, seems to be on a par with others.

II. SOME DIG BENEATH THE SURFACE, BUT NOT DEEP ENOUGH.
   1. Some intellectual lives pierce the surface without going deep enough; pseudo scientists; half-baked theologians, etc.
   2. Some moral lives go below the surface, but not deep enough.

III. The Only Sure Foundation Is Christ, the Rock.
   1. To rest on him we must dig deep.
   2. Only as we build on him do we experience satisfaction and security.
   3. Building on Christ, we build for eternity.

180. BEFORE AND AFTER

"And he went his way, and published throughout the whole city how great things Jesus had done unto him." *Luke 8:39*

I. Before
   1. No home
   2. Lived among the dead
   3. Wanted nothing to do with Jesus
   4. No rest, day or night
   5. Unclothed
   6. Injured himself

II. After
   1. Sitting (relaxed)
   2. Clothed in his right mind
   3. Wanted the companionship of Jesus
   4. Testified for Jesus

181. FAITH REWARDED

"He said unto her, Daughter, be of good comfort: thy faith hath made thee whole; go in peace." *Luke 8:48*

The woman's faith was:
1. Secretly cherished
2. Courageously shown
3. Immediately discovered
4. Humbly confessed
5. Happily rewarded

—Van Doren

182. THE GREAT PHYSICIAN

"He . . . healed them that had need of healing." *Luke 9:11*

I. His Skill
   1. Knows no limitations
   2. Has the healing touch

II. His Insight
   1. "He knew what was in man."
   2. "The Lord looketh on the heart."

III. His Availability
   1. "Whosoever will may come."
   2. Day or night; anywhere

IV. The Cost
   1. "Without money and without price"
   2. "The gift of God is eternal life."

V. His Sympathy with Sufferers
   1. "Moved with compassion"
   2. "The Comforter"

VI. Eventually
   1. No more pain
   2. Eternal life

183. TRANSFIGURATION THROUGH PRAYER

"As he prayed, the fashion of his countenance was altered." *Luke 9:29*

I. Prayer Produces a Calmness, a Serenity, a Peace the World Can Neither Give nor Take Away.

II. Prayer Engenders Courage. (The prayer in Gethsemane gave Christ the courage he showed before Pilate and on the cross.)

III. Prayer Transfigures the Face and Reveals the Inward Life.

(It is when our faces are turned heavenward that God's sunshine lights upon them.)

—T. J. Madden

184. GETTING RID OF THE DEVIL

"Even the devils are subject unto us through thy name." *Luke 10:17*

There are certain things we can do to force Satan out of our hearts.

I. Sometimes We Can Think Him Out.
   1. "Come now, and let us *reason* together, saith the

Lord: though your sins be as scarlet," etc.

2. The prodigal son did a lot of sober thinking.

II. WE MAY FREEZE HIM OUT.

1. The reason Satan lingers in many a heart is that he receives a warm welcome there.
2. It has been said that "Satan is too much of a gentleman to stay where he isn't wanted."

III. WE MAY GET HIM OUT BY FORCIBLE EVICTION.

1. Landlords cannot always do as they please with their tenants, but we still have the say as to whether Satan can make his permanent abode in our hearts.
2. "Get thee hence, Satan."

IV. PRAYER CREATES AN UNHEALTHY ATMOSPHERE FOR SATAN.

1. "And Satan trembles when
   he sees
   The weakest saint upon
   his knees."
   —Cowper
2. Prayer summons a higher power to our assistance.
3. Jesus often cast out demons.

V. THE SIMPLEST, SUREST WAY TO GET SATAN OUT IS TO BID JESUS TO COME IN.

1. The more room we give Christ, the less room there will be for Satan.
2. "For this purpose the Son of God was manifested, that he might destroy the works of the devil." I John 3:8.

185. WHAT IS PRAYER?

"Lord, teach us to pray."
Luke 11:1

Prayer is:
1. Talking to God
2. Listening to God
3. Thinking with God
4. Submitting to God
5. Living and working in the presence of God

—J. Gordon Howard

186. BIRDS OF A FEATHER

"He said unto them, take heed, and beware of covetousness."
Luke 12:15

An old proverb has it that "birds of a feather will gather together." Another is, "A man is known by the company he keeps."

The principle may also be applied to words. The sin of covetousness must indeed be a very serious one, to judge by the company the word keeps.

In I Cor. 6:9-10 we find the word "covetous" keeping some very bad company.

"Know ye not that the unrighteous shall not inherit the kingdom of God? Be not deceived: neither fornicators, nor idolators, nor adulterers, nor effeminate, nor abusers of themselves with mankind, nor thieves, nor *covetous*, nor drunkards, nor revilers, nor extortioners, shall inherit the kingdom of God."

187. YOU CAN'T EVADE RESPONSIBILITY

"Unto whomsoever much is given, of him shall be much required." *Luke 12:48*

Also read Matt. 25.

The entire twenty-fifth chapter of Matthew is taken up with three parables, all of which teach the impossibility of evading responsibility in the sight of God.

I. THE PARABLE OF THE VIRGINS CONDEMNS NEGLECT.

1. The foolish virgins had good intentions, but they neglected their duties until too late.
2. "The road to hell is paved with good intentions."

II. THE PARABLE OF THE TALENTS CONDEMNS INDOLENCE.
1. The "one-talent" man just "couldn't be bothered."
2. "If you want something done, ask a busy man to do it."

III. THE PARABLE OF THE JUDGEMENT CONDEMNS SELFISHNESS.
1. The persons Jesus condemned were not guilty of doing wrong, but failing to do right.
2. Sins of omission are as serious as those of commission.

Application: The text

188. THE PRODIGAL COMES HOME

"I will arise and go to my father." *Luke 15:18*

Read Luke 15:11-24.

I. DOWNWARD COURSE
1. Restless: "Father, give me."
2. Rebellious: "gathered all together."
3. Revelry: "wasted his substance."
4. Ruin: "spent all, . . . in want. . . . No man gave unto him."

II. UPWARD AND HOMEWARD COURSE
1. Reflects: "He came to himself."
2. Repents: "Hired servants of my father's have bread . . . and I perish."
3. Resolves: "I will arise."
4. Returns: "He arose."
5. Received: "His father saw him, and had compassion."
6. Reconciled: "His father . . . kissed him."
7. Re-instated: "Bring forth the best robe," etc.
8. Rejoicing: "This my son . . . is alive again."

—*London City Missionary*

189. DIVES AND LAZARUS

"There was a certain rich man. . . . And there was a certain beggar named Lazarus." *Luke 16:19, 20*

1. Two men—one rich, the other poor

2. Two lives—one Christless, the other Christian

3. Two deaths—one in sin, the other in faith

4. Two destinies—one in hell, the other in heaven

190. THE CONVERSION OF ZACCHAEUS

"Zacchaeus stood, and said unto the Lord; Behold, Lord, the half of my goods I give to the poor; and if I have taken any thing from any man by false accusation, I restore him fourfold."

Luke 19:8

Read Luke 19:2-10.

Of the many conversions recorded in the Bible, there are no two alike. None is more interesting than that of Zacchaeus. Let us consider:

I. ZACCHAEUS SEEKING JESUS
1. Who was Zacchaeus? (Verse 2.)
2. Zacchaeus desires to *see* Jesus. (Verse 3.)
3. Zacchaeus *seeks* Jesus. (Verse 4.)
4. Zacchaeus is hindered from seeing Jesus.
   a. By the crowd
   b. By his physical handicaps

II. ZACCHAEUS RECEIVING JESUS
1. Saw the Master; heard the challenge (verse 5)
2. Lost no time (verse 6)
3. A joyful experience (verse 6)

III. ZACCHAEUS CONFESSING JESUS
1. Openly—before family and friends (verses 7-8)
2. His heart made generous (verse 8)

3. Old accounts settled (verse 8)

IV. Zacchaeus' Conversion Confirmed

1. Verses 9-10.

191. TEARS FOR A DOOMED CITY

"When he was come near, he beheld the city, and wept over it."
Luke 19:41

It is a sadly significant fact that many of the causes of the decline and destruction of ancient Jerusalem are in evidence in many of our modern cities.

1. Formalism
2. Skepticism
3. Ingratitude for special privileges
4. Mammonism
5. Poverty unheeded
6. Social impurity
7. Intemperance

—J. O. Davies

192. THE UPPER ROOM

"He shall shew you a large upper room furnished: there make ready."
Luke 22:12

I. The Room Itself

1. Probable description
2. Thought to be in the home of John Mark

II. The Use Made of It by Jesus and His Disciples

1. Passover feast
2. Lord's Supper instituted
3. Jesus there taught his deepest truths
4. From there to Gethsemane; Calvary
5. Here Jesus fulfilled his promise to be with just a few who gathered in his name.
6. Disciples used the room for prayerful preparation for Pentecost.

III. We, Too, May Have Access to the Upper Room.

1. Door no longer barred
2. Whosoever will may enter.
3. Fellowship with Christ and kindred spirits

193. DEATHBED REPENTANCE

"Lord, remember me when thou comest into thy kingdom."
Luke 23:42

1. At the throne of grace only grace counts.
2. Last-minute confessions are better than none.
3. Ecclesiastical formalities do not count under some circumstances.
4. Truly penitent souls are saved by Him who can "save to the uttermost."

—Walter D. Mehrling

194. THE EMMAUS STORY

"It came to pass, that, while they communed together and reasoned, Jesus himself drew near, and went with them."
Luke 24:15

I. Jesus Was Unconventional.

1. No formality. He "drew near, and went with them."
2. Always with the few who gather in his name

II. Jesus Fraternized with the Poor as Well as the Rich.

1. Alphaeus and Cleopas were probably very poor. It made no difference to Jesus.
2. No home too humble for him to enter

III. Jesus Used His Social Genius to Talk Religion.

1. Always ready to explain problems in the light of Scripture
2. He knew his Bible.

IV. Jesus Doesn't Press His Company on Anyone.

1. "He made as though he would have gone further."
2. "Jesus is too much of a gentleman to go where he isn't wanted."

3. He stands at the door and knocks, but he doesn't crash the door.

V. JESUS WARMS THE HEARTS OF THOSE WHO BID HIM ENTER.

1. "Did not our heart burn within us, while he talked with us by the way?"
2. Many hearts, like John Wesley's have been "strangely warmed."

195. IT ALL HAPPENED IN ONE DAY

"He saith unto them, Come and see. They came and saw."

John 1:39

1. Looking upon Jesus (John 1:36)
2. Following Jesus (John 1:37)
3. Abiding with Jesus (John 1:39)
4. Bringing others to Jesus (John 1:42)

—*Bible Helps for Busy Men*

196. ANDREW—THE PERSONAL WORKER

"He first findeth his own brother Simon, and saith unto him, We have found the Messias. . . . And he brought him to Jesus."

—*John 1:41, 42*

Andrew has been called "the patron saint of personal workers." Every time his name appears in the Bible we find him bringing someone to Christ.

I. FIRST APPEARANCE—BRINGING HIS BROTHER TO CHRIST

1. Text
2. What a day's work that was, when Simon Peter was brought to the Lord!
3. Many great Christian leaders were first brought to Christ by obscure Sunday-school teachers or lay workers.

II. SECOND APPEARANCE—BRINGING A LAD TO CHRIST

1. Result: a multitude fed
2. Never underestimate the potentialities of a boy.

III. THIRD MENTION—BRINGING SOME GENTILES TO CHRIST

1. Greeks: "We would see Jesus." Philip enlisted Andrew's aid in the matter. Andrew knew just what to do.
2. Evangelism crosses racial barriers.

Application: Andrew was interested in every phase of evangelism. Home (his brother); child (the lad); mass (assisted at Pentecost); missionary (the Greeks).

What an example Andrew has set for all who profess discipleship to Christ!

197. JESUS THE MIND READER

"He knew what was in man."

John 2:25

1. When he was tempted by Satan, Jesus saw through the lying promises that were made.
2. When he called the fishermen, he knew what they could become if they followed him.
3. In the rich young ruler he saw one who could become a powerful leader, if consecrated.
4. He saw the hypocrisy in the heart of Judas before it came to the surface.
5. In Nathanael he saw "an Israelite in whom was no guile."
6. In the accusers of the woman taken in adultery he saw men as guilty as she.
7. In the scribes and Pharisees he saw whited sepulchres concealing corruption.

198. THE GREAT TEACHER

"Rabbi, we know that thou art a teacher come from God."

John 3:2

I. CERTAIN FEATURES OF CHRIST'S

TEACHING CANNOT BE IMITATED.
1. His originality
2. Teaching by miracles
3. His authority

II. CERTAIN FEATURES OF CHRIST'S TEACHING ALL SHOULD IMITATE.
1. His naturalness
2. His suggestiveness
3. His catholicity
4. His spirituality
5. His tenderness
6. His faithfulness
7. His consistency
8. His devoutness

—*Biblical Encyclopedia*

199. REGENERATION

"Except a man be born again, he cannot see the kingdom of God."
John 3:3

1. A radical change (II Cor. 5:17)
2. A necessary change (John 3:3)
3. A spiritual change (John 3:6)
4. By the Holy Spirit (Tit. 3:5-6)
5. Its manner (Acts 16:31)
6. Its evidences (I John 3:14, 24)

—M. G. Price

200. FOUR STEPS IN THE NEW BIRTH

"Ye must be born again."
John 3:7

1. Conviction (John 16:8-9)
2. Repentance (II Cor. 7:10)
3. Faith (John 6:37)
4. Forgiveness (I John 1:9)

—William D. Laumaster

201. SALVATION

"God so loved the world, that he gave his only begotten Son, that whosoever believeth in him should not perish, but have everlasting life."
John 3:16

I. THE ORIGIN OF SALVATION—"GOD"

II. THE CAUSE OF SALVATION—"LOVED"

III. THE SUBJECT OF SALVATION — MANKIND — "THE WORLD"

IV. THE NATURE OF SALVATION—GRATUITOUS—"GAVE"

V. THE BASIS OF SALVATION—JESUS CHRIST—"HIS ONLY BEGOTTEN SON"

VI. THE EXTENT OF SALVATION—INDIVIDUAL — "WHOSOEVER"

VII. THE CONDITION OF SALVATION—FAITH—"BELIEVETH"

VIII. THE TIME OF SALVATION—NOW—"HAVE"

IX. THE RESULT OF SALVATION
1. Negatively—"should not perish"
2. Positively—"have everlasting life"

—Samuel Falcao

202. THE THINKER

"Never man spake like this man."
John 7:46

Jesus brought to the world:

1. A new aspect of God—as Father
2. A new view of man—all men brethren
3. A new code of ethics—the law of the second mile
4. A new vision of the beyond—"In my Father's house are many mansions."

203. CHRIST THE DOOR

"Verily, verily, I say unto you, I am the door."
John 10:7

I. JESUS IS THE DOOR TO THE FOLD OF SAFETY.
1. The fold protected the sheep from the icy winds, wild animals, robbers.
2. Christ protects us from dangers that assail the soul.

II. HE IS THE DOOR TO THE STOREHOUSE OF GOSPEL BLESSINGS.

1. "Ye through his poverty might be rich." II Cor. 8:9.

III. He Is the Door to God and Heaven.

1. "No man cometh unto the Father, but by me."
2. Jesus is the door to that "house not made with hands, eternal in the heavens."

204. KNOWING VS. DOING

"If ye know these things, happy are ye if ye do them." *John 13:17*

I. Knowledge of Religion Alone Will Not Make One Happy.

1. Mere knowledge does not make one better.
2. Mere knowledge does not insure salvation.
3. The possession of knowledge makes one's case worse.

II. It Is the Practice of Religion That Makes One Happy.

1. A reproof to those who know much but do little
2. An exhortation to all who have a practical religion

—T. Watson

205. THE MARK OF A CHRISTIAN

"By this shall all men know that ye are my disciples, if ye have love one to another." *John 13:35*

I. Love Is the Sign and Seal of True Christianity.

1. It is taught in the incarnation of the Saviour.
2. It is proclaimed in every act of his life.
3. It is manifested in his death upon the cross.
4. It is prominent in all his teachings.

II. The Nature and Character of Christian Love.

1. It must be implanted in our hearts by the Holy Spirit.
2. Impartial
3. Sincere
4. Practical

—Clericus

206. OUR HEAVENLY HOME

"If I go and prepare a place for you, I will come again, and receive you unto myself; that where I am, there ye may be also." *John 14:3*

Our heavenly home is:

I. A Prepared Home

1. "I go to prepare. . . . John 14:2.
2. "Heaven is a prepared place for a prepared people."

II. A Pure Home

1. "Blessed are the pure in heart: for they shall see God." Matt. 5:8.
2. "These . . . have washed their robes, and made them white in the blood of the Lamb." Rev. 7:14.

III. A Populated Home

1. "A great multitude, which no man could number." Rev. 7:9.
2. "A great cloud of witnesses"

IV. A Protected Home

1. God is in the midst. Rev. 7:15.
2. "God is our refuge and strength."

V. A Pleasant Home

1. Happiness belongs to the inhabitants.
2. "God shall wipe away all tears." Rev. 7:17.

—Neill G. Stevens

207. JOY OF THE LORD

"These things have I spoken unto you, that my joy might remain in you, and that your joy might be full." *John 15:11*

I. It Is God's Will That All Men Shall Be Joyful.

(Joyful = joy full)

II. Why Many Never Find This Joy.

(They do not seek it where it

can be found, which is in Christ.)

III. THE JOY OF THE LORD LINGERS IN THE HEART.
(“That my joy might remain in you.” Earth’s joys are fleeting.)

IV. FULNESS OF JOY IN HEAVEN.
(“In thy presence is fulness of joy; at thy right hand there are pleasures for evermore.” Ps. 16:11.)

208. WHY JESUS WENT AWAY

“It is expedient for you that I go away.” *John 16:7*

Why did Jesus go away?

I. “TO PREPARE A PLACE FOR YOU”

II. THAT THE COMFORTER MIGHT COME
(He went away physically so that his spiritual presence might be realized.)

III. SO THAT ALL MEN EVERYWHERE MIGHT HAVE HIS PRESENCE WITH THEM
(No longer limited by a human body, he is omnipresent.)

IV. THAT MEN MIGHT WALK BY FAITH

209. PETER DENIES HIS LORD

“Then saith the damsel that kept the door unto Peter, Art not thou also one of this man’s disciples? He saith, I am not.” *John 18:17*

Peter’s denial of Christ was a grievous sin. The disciple disowned his Master, the servant of his Lord.

I. THE ELEMENTS OF THE DENIAL
1. Falsehood
2. Cowardice
3. Profanity
4. Persistence

II. THE DENIAL BY ONE WHO HAD HAD SUPERIOR ADVANTAGES
1. Peter had had years of close fellowship with Christ.
2. He had been warned repeatedly.
3. He had made strong professions of loyalty.
4. The emergency should have called forth heroism instead of cowardice.

III. MITIGATING CIRCUMSTANCES
1. It was sudden.
2. It was brief.
3. It was never repeated.

IV. THE CHIEF CAUSES OF THE DENIAL
1. Self-confidence
2. Blindness to near danger
3. Negligence of precautions
4. Fear of derision

—Braithwaite

210. THE THREE CROSSES

“. . . on either side one, and Jesus in the midst.” *John 19:18*

I. THE SAVED THIEF
(Sin in him, not on him)

II. THE LORD JESUS
(Sin on Him, not in Him)

III. THE UNSAVED THIEF
(Sin in him and on him)

—*Expositor*

211. SECRET DISCIPLESHIP

“Joseph of Arimathaea, being a disciple of Jesus, but secretly.” *John 19:38*

I. THE REALITY OF HIDDEN DISCIPLESHIP
1. Many names are written in the book of life that are not recorded upon church registers.
2. Many names on church registers are not in the “Lamb’s Book of Life.”

II. THE UNSATISFACTORINESS OF HIDDEN DISCIPLESHIP
1. It violates the finest instinct of the Christian heart.
2. It is contrary to the genius of Christianity.
3. It is contrary to the development of Christian character.

III. HIDDEN DISCIPLESHIP CAN BECOME OPEN.
1. Joseph went boldly to Pilate and begged the body of Jesus.

—W. L. Watkinson

212. CHRISTIAN GLADNESS

"Then were the disciples glad when they saw the Lord."

John 20:20

They were glad:
1. For his sake
2. For their own sake
3. For the sake of the world

213. THE DEVELOPMENT OF POWER

"Ye shall receive power, after that the Holy Ghost is come upon you." *Acts 1:8*

1. Power (Acts 1:8).
2. Great power (Acts 4:33).
3. Mighty power (Eph. 1:19).
4. Excellent power (II Cor. 4:7).
5. Exceeding great power (Eph. 1:19).
6. Divine power (II Pet. 1:3).
7. Eternal power (Rom. 1:20).
8. Glorious power (Col. 1:11).

—T. B.

214. CHRIST AND HEAVEN

"And when he had spoken these things, while they beheld, he was taken up; and a cloud received him out of their sight." *Acts 1:9*

1. From heaven he came. (John 3:13; I Cor. 15:47.)
2. Of heaven he spoke. (Matt. 5:12.)
3. To heaven he pointed. (Matt. 4:17; John 17:24.)
4. To heaven he ascended. (Heb. 10:12; Acts 2:33.)
5. To heaven he invites us. (Matt. 6:19-21; Rev. 3:21.)
6. In heaven he prepares for us. (John 14:2.)

—*Curiosities of the Bible*

215. IT MIGHT HAVE BEEN

". . . Judas, which was guide to them that took Jesus."

Acts 1:16

"For of all sad words of tongue or pen,
The saddest are these: 'It might have been!'"

—Whittier

I. JUDAS MIGHT HAVE BEEN A CHRISTIAN LEADER.
(He was "guide to them that took Jesus.")

II. JUDAS OUGHT TO HAVE RECEIVED THE HOLY GHOST.
("The devil . . . put into the heart of Judas." John 13:2.)

III. JUDAS OUGHT TO HAVE LIVED THE RISEN LIFE IN CHRIST.
(He died a suicide.)

IV. JUDAS OUGHT TO HAVE LIVED IN THE LIGHT OF CHRIST.
("He . . . went immediately out: and it was night.")

V. JUDAS MIGHT HAVE BEEN A MISSIONARY AND GAINED TERRITORY FOR THE CHURCH.
(He left "Aceldama, . . . the field of blood.")

216. PRIMITIVE CHRISTIANITY

"They continued stedfastly in the apostles' doctrine and fellowship." *Acts 2:42*

Read Acts 2:42-47.

I. THEIR CONSTANCY
("They continued." Verses 42, 46.)

II. THEIR FELLOWSHIP
("With one accord." Verse 46.)

III. THEIR WEEKDAY RELIGION
("Daily." Verse 46.)

IV. THEIR SHARED LIVES
("All things common." Verse 44.)

V. THEIR DOCTRINE, THE ATONEMENT
("Breaking bread." Verse 46.)

VI. THEIR HAPPINESS

("Gladness . . . praising." Verses 46, 47.)

VII. THEIR EVANGELISM
("The Lord added to the church daily." Verse 47.)

217. OBEDIENCE PAYS OFF

"We ought to obey God rather than men." *Acts 5:29*

Why?

I. BECAUSE HE IS SUPREME
1. Creator
2. King of kings
3. Father

II. BECAUSE OF HIS INFINITE WISDOM AND GOODNESS
1. "If ye . . . know how to give good gifts unto your children, how much more shall your Father which is in heaven give good things to them that ask him?" Matt. 7:11.
2. "All things work together for good to them that love God." Rom. 8:28.

III. BECAUSE WE PROFIT THROUGH OBEDIENCE
1. "Godliness is profitable unto all things, having promise of the life that now is, and of that which is to come" (I Tim. 4:8).

218. WE ARE WITNESSES

"We are his witnesses of these things; and so is also the Holy Ghost, whom God hath given to them that obey him." *Acts 5:32*

I. THE SUBJECT MATTER OF THE WITNESSING
1. "These things." The crucifixion, resurrection, and ascension of Christ. (Verses 30-31.)

II. THE CHARACTER OF THE WITNESSING
1. Boldness
2. Humility
3. Common sense
4. Continuity; generation after generation

III. WHY WITNESS FOR CHRIST?
1. The instinct of self-preservation
2. Sense of gratitude
3. Desire to share Christ with others

—G. Barlow

219. FIGHTING GOD

"Ye do always resist the Holy Ghost." *Acts 7:51*

I. THE OFFICE OF THE HOLY GHOST
1. Convincing
2. Entreating
3. Admonishing
4. Threatening

II. THE MEANS HE USES
1. The Word
2. Examples
3. Conscience
4. Providential dealings

III. WAYS MEN RESIST HIM
1. Inattention
2. Procrastination
3. Contradiction

220. IMPROVISED PULPITS

"They that were scattered abroad went every where preaching the word." *Acts 8:4*

1. On the streets of Jerusalem (Acts 2:14)
2. At the gate of the Temple (Acts 3:12)
3. In the council chamber (Acts 5:29)
4. In a chariot in the desert (Acts 8:30)
5. In the synagogue (Acts 9:20; 13:14)
6. In the house of Cornelius (Acts 10:24)
7. At a river side in Philippi (Acts 16:13)
8. In an inner prison (Acts 16:31)
9. In a jailor's house (Acts 16:32)
10. On Mars' Hill in Athens (Acts 17:22)

11. In the school of Tyrannus (Acts 19:9)
12. From house to house (Acts 20:20)
13. Before Felix the governor (Acts 24:24)
14. Before King Agrippa (Acts 26:1)
15. In a hired house (Acts 28:30)

---

221. AN IDEAL SOUL WINNER

"Then Philip opened his mouth, and . . . preached unto him Jesus."
Acts 8:35

I. Philip Had the Confidence of the Church.
(Chosen as a deacon—Acts 6:5)

II. Philip a Good Man and Full of the Holy Spirit.
(Acts 6:3; 8:29)

III. Intelligent
("Full of . . . wisdom"—Acts 6:3)

IV. Ready to Serve
("He arose and went." Acts 8:27.)

V. Tactful in Approaching His Prospect.
("Understandest thou what . . . ?" Acts 8:30.)

VI. Knew His Bible, and Knew Christ.
("Began at the same scripture, and preached unto him Jesus." Acts 8:35.)

VII. Got Results.
(The eunuch was happily converted and baptized. Acts 8:36-39.)

VIII. One Victory Didn't Satisfy Him.
("Preached in all the cities." Acts 8:40.)

---

222. CONVERSION OF CORNELIUS

"Cornelius waited for them, and had called together his kinsmen and near friends." *Acts 10:24*

Read Acts 10.

I. Cornelius Was Doing the Will of God So Far as He Knew It.
1. Devout; feared God
2. Taught his household
3. Gave alms
4. Prayed

II. He Earnestly Desired to Know More About Spiritual Things.

III. He Obeyed God's Directions About How to Learn More.
1. Sent for God's messenger
2. Heard the Word attentively
3. Opened his heart to the Holy Spirit

IV. He Called His Friends Together, That They, Too, Might Receive the Blessing.

V. He United with the Church Without Delay.

VI. He Kept on Trying to Learn More: by Desiring Peter to Tarry.

—Henderson

---

223. PETER'S SERMON IN THE HOUSE OF CORNELIUS

"To him give all the prophets witness, that through his name whosoever believeth in him shall receive remission of sins."
Acts 10:43

Read Acts 10:34-43.

1. God's universal *acceptance* of the human race (verses 34-35)
2. God's universal *tidings of peace* to the human race (verses 36-38)
3. God's universal *witnesses* to the human race (verses 39-42*a*)
4. God's universal *judge* of the human race (verses 42*b*-43*a*)
5. God's universal *invitation* to the human race (verse 43*b*)

—R. W. Van Anda

---

224. CHRISTIANS CLASSIFIED

"The disciples were called Christians first in Antioch."
Acts 11:26

I. JAWBONE CHRISTIANS
   1. Plenty of talk, but little more
   2. Many are opinionated, dogmatic, arrogant.
   3. Jesus condemned those who were argumentative, emphasizing the letter of the law, ignoring the spirit of it.

II. WISHBONE CHRISTIANS
   1. Always hoping, desiring, even praying, for things to happen for the advancement of the Church and the Kingdom, yet doing nothing to bring things to pass

III. BACKBONE CHRISTIANS
   1. Courage of conviction; taking a stand for Christ and the Church, in season, out of season
   2. They get under the burdens.
   3. They see the problems and needs, and do something about them.

225. WHY MISSIONS?

"A vision appeared to Paul in the night; There stood a man of Macedonia, and prayed him, saying, Come over into Macedonia and help us." *Acts 16:9*

Why missions?

I. THE SOUL'S EXPERIENCE IN CHRIST
   1. Gratitude for our own redemption should prompt us to share it with others.
   2. "The Christ we will not share we cannot keep."

II. THE WORLD'S GREAT NEED OF CHRIST
   1. To behold a world in tragic need and have the answer to that need, yet withhold it, is to be something else—and less—than Christian.
   2. Criminal negligence

III. THE COMMAND OF CHRIST—"GO YE INTO ALL THE WORLD AND PREACH THE GOSPEL."
   1. The command is peremptory.
   2. Obedience should be immediate, without hesitation.
   3. Obedience should be as prompt as that of soldiers to a commander's orders.

226. THE CONVERSION OF LYDIA

"A certain woman named Lydia, a seller of purple, of the city of Thyatira, which worshipped God, heard us: whose heart the Lord opened, that she attended unto the things which were spoken of Paul." *Acts 16:14*

Read Acts 16:13-15.

I. SHE WAS IN A GOOD PLACE TO BE CONVERTED.
   1. A prayer meeting (verse 13).
   2. Environment has its part in conversion.

II. SHE HAD AN OPEN MIND AND HEART.
   1. Heart opened (verse 14).
   2. Attentive (verse 14).

III. SHE PROFESSED HER FAITH AND ACCEPTANCE OF CHRIST
   1. Baptized (verse 15).
   2. Influenced her household (verse 15).

IV. ESTABLISHED A CHRISTIAN HOME
   1. Invited Paul and Silas (verse 15).
   2. Her home a refuge for the persecuted (verse 40).

227. THE NEARNESS OF GOD

"He is not far from each one of us." *Acts 17:27 (A.S.V.)*

1. He is near to us in his essential presence.

2. He is near to us in the manifestation of divine pity.

3. He is near to us in his spiritual provision.

4. He is near to us in the workings of his providence.

—T. J. Madden

228. IN HIM WE LIVE

"In him we live, and move, and have our being." *Acts 17:28*

Paul here sets forth the threefold relationship of believers to Christ:

I. "In Him We Live."
   1. Without Christ we are "dead in trespasses and sins."
   2. "As in Adam all die, even so in Christ shall all be made alive." Paul.

II. In Him We "Move."
   1. No standstill in the Christian life
   2. If we are Christians, we are on the march.
   3. Christians, like their Master, must go "about, doing good."

III. In Him We "Have Our Being."
   1. "Rooted and grounded" in Christ
   2. "I am the vine, ye are the branches."

229. APOLLOS—A GOOD MINISTER

"He mightily convinced the Jews, and that publickly, shewing by the Scriptures that Jesus was Christ." *Acts 18:28*

Read Acts 18:24-28.

I. "An Eloquent Man" (verse 24).

II. "Mighty in the Scriptures" (verse 24).
   (He knew his Bible.)

III. He "Was Instructed in the Way of the Lord" (verse 25).
   (Christian education.)

IV. "Fervent in the Spirit" (verse 25).
   (Sincerity; earnestness; devoutness.)

V. "Began to Speak Boldly" (verse 26).
   (Had the courage of conviction.)

VI. Was Teachable (verse 26).

VII. An Effective Teacher (verse 28).

230. FILLED WITH THE SPIRIT

"Have ye received the Holy Ghost since ye believed?" *Acts 19:2*

The Christian should:

1. Be filled with the Spirit (Eph. 5:18).
2. Pray in the spirit (Jude 20; Eph. 6:18).
3. Sing in the Spirit (Eph. 5:19).
4. Worship in the Spirit (John 4:23; Phil. 3:3).
5. Walk in the Spirit (Gal. 5:16).
6. Be led by the Spirit (Gal. 5:18).
7. Remember his body is the temple of the Spirit (I Cor. 6:19).

—J. M. H.

231. PAUL'S MINISTRY AT EPHESUS

"I have not shunned to declare unto you all the counsel of God." *Acts 20:27*

Read Acts 20:17-35.

Paul's ministry was:

1. A wise ministry (verses 18-19)
2. A weeping ministry (verse 19)
3. A working ministry (verses 20-21)
4. A watchful ministry (verses 24-27)
5. A warning ministry (verses 28-31)
6. A well-rounded ministry (verses 34-35)

—Ezra S. Gerig

232. THE INCARNATION OF GOD

". . . concerning his Son Jesus Christ our Lord, which was made of the seed of David according to the flesh and declared to be the Son of God with power." *Rom. 1:3-4*

1. The Incarnation can have nothing like it, or parallel to it, while the world lasts.

2. The Incarnation was the turning point in the history of the world.

3. In the Incarnation we see how God fulfills the promises he makes, and the hopes he raises.

—Dean Church

233. CALLED TO BE SAINTS

". . . to all that be in Rome, beloved of God, called to be saints."
Rom. 1:7

We are very apt to regard the apostolic saints as though they were "saints" in a more especial manner than the other children of God. Their holiness is attainable even by us.

I. THEY LIVED WITH JESUS.
II. THEY LIVED FOR JESUS.
III. THEY GREW LIKE JESUS.

Application: If we live by the same spirit and formula, our saintliness will soon be apparent.

—Charles H. Spurgeon

234. WHY BE ASHAMED?

"I am not ashamed of the gospel of Christ: for it is the power of God unto salvation to every one that believeth; to the Jew first, and also to the Greek."
Rom. 1:16

I. THE GREATEST POSITION
"Not ashamed"
II. THE GREATEST REASON
"It is the power of God unto salvation."
III. THE GREATEST SCOPE
"To every one that believeth"
IV. THE GREATEST IMPARTIALITY
"Jew and Greek"

—D. Van Dyke

235. WANT TO GET RICH?

"Despisest thou the riches of his goodness . . . ?" *Rom. 2:4*

Riches of:

1. Goodness (Rom. 2:4)
2. Grace (Eph. 1:7)
3. Mercy (Eph. 2:4)
4. Glory (Phil. 4:10)
5. God (Rom. 11:33)

—*Evangelistic Cyclopedia*

236. THE IMPARTIALITY OF GOD

"There is no respect of persons with God." *Rom. 2:11*

1. A *terrible truth* for all the ungodly among the great
2. A *comforting truth* for all the pious among the poor

—*Biblical Encyclopedia*

237. THE AUTHORITY OF THE BOOK

"What saith the scripture?"
Rom. 4:3

I. AS REVELATION
(Without it man has no light on the nature of God, God's relations to man, the method of reconciliation, and immortality.)
II. AS A COUNSELOR
(The Scripture is an infallible guide.)
III. AS A STANDARD
(The authoritative standard of faith and practice)
IV. AS A JUDGE
(The Scripture will judge those to whom it has been given at the last day.)

—J. W. Burn

238. THE PARDON OF SIN

"Blessed are they whose iniquities are forgiven, and whose sins are covered." *Rom. 4:7*

I. TO PARDON SIN IS GOD'S PREROGATIVE.
II. PARDON OF SIN IS A COVERING OF SIN.
III. GOD'S ACT OF PARDONING SIN IS:
1. Extensive
2. Perfect
3. Full

4. Final

IV. The Great Blessedness of Those Whose Iniquity Is Pardoned.

—Burkitt

239. THE GOSPEL IN A NUTSHELL

"Christ died for us." *Rom. 5:8*

I. The Subject: "Christ"
   1. The divine Son of the living God
   2. "The just for the unjust"

II. The Predicate: "Died"
   1. Voluntarily
   2. Ignominiously

III. The Object: "Us"
   1. Not just for his generation or race, but for all mankind, everywhere, and in all generations; and that includes us.
   2. We are the beneficiaries.

240. HEIRS OF GOD

"If children, then heirs; heirs of God, and joint-heirs with Christ." *Rom. 8:17*

1. No inheritance without sonship
2. No sonship without spiritual birth
3. No spiritual birth without Christ
4. No Christ without faith

241. A COMFORTING PHILOSOPHY

"We know that all things work together for good to them that love God." *Rom. 8:28*

When we sincerely love God and are striving as best we know how to do the will of God, we may depend upon it that "all things" will work out to the blessing of our lives.

I. "All Things" Act Energetically for Our Good.
   (They "work.")

II. "All Things" Act Harmoniously for Our Good.
   (They work "together.")

III. "All Things" Work Beneficially.
   ("For good.")

Application: In the way of God's will there is peace, power, joy; here and hereafter.

242. IN THE MINORITY

"If God be for us, who can be against us?" *Rom. 8:31*

Men in minorities:

1. Noah, while building the ark
2. Joseph, sold into slavery; imprisoned
3. Gideon and his "Three hundred"
4. Elijah, in his contest with the prophets of Baal
5. David, fighting although ridiculed even by his brethren
6. Martin Luther, nailing his theses to the door
7. Paul, in chains
8. Jesus Christ, nailed to the cross

Well has it been said: "One man and God constitute a majority."

243. THE INEFFECTUAL BIBLE

"Not as though the word of God hath taken none effect." *Rom. 9:6*

I. In Some the Word of God Takes No Effect.
   1. They do not repent.
   2. They do not believe.
   3. They are not saved.

II. Their Ineffectual Use of the Bible Is Not Proof of Its Ineffectiveness with Others.
   1. With many it is "the power of God unto salvation."
   2. Food uneaten has no value.

III. In the Judgment the Ineffectiveness of the Bible Will Be Obvious.
   1. To sinners
   2. To saints

244. THE PLACE OF PREACHING

"How shall they hear without a preacher?" *Rom. 10:14*

1. Preaching is God's ordained method of communicating divine knowledge.
2. Without divine knowledge men cannot believe.
3. Without faith men cannot call upon God.
4. Without calling upon God they cannot be saved.

—J. Lyth

245. THE MERCIES OF GOD

"I beseech you therefore, brethren, by the mercies of God, that ye present your bodies a living sacrifice, holy, acceptable unto God, which is your reasonable service." *Rom. 12:1*

The mercies of God are as numberless as the sands of the sea. For a quick and comprehensive summary of God's mercies we may think of the five senses.

I. SIGHT
   1. What a blessing to be able to see our friends, the flowers, the trees, the skies, the sunsets, the rainbows, the birds, the beauties of our Father's world!
   2. What a blessing to be able to see the pathway, the printed page, the emotions registered in the faces of our loved ones!

II. SOUND
   1. Music
   2. Voices
   3. Messages
   4. Warnings
   5. Conversations

III. SMELL
   1. Flowers; new-mown hay
   2. Savory food
   3. The warning odors of poisons, etc.

IV. TASTE

V. TOUCH

246. BE NOT CONFORMED

"Be not conformed to this world." *Rom. 12:2*

I. CONFORMITY IS NOT:
   1. Rational enjoyment of innocent pleasures
   2. Needed attention to legitimate work
   3. Giving proper play to natural impulses

II. CONFORMITY MEANS:
   1. Accepting worldly standards
   2. Immoderate pursuit of worldly prizes
   3. Enthronement of material things
   4. Being lovers of pleasure rather than of God

—*The Pastor His Own Evangelist*

247. ASK A BUSY MAN

". . . not slothful in business; . . . serving the Lord." *Rom. 12:11*

When God wants a great servant, he calls a busy man. Scripture and history attest this truth.

When challenged to serve:

Moses was busy with his flocks at Horeb.

Gideon was threshing wheat.

David was out in the field with his father's sheep.

Elisha was busy plowing with twelve yoke of oxen.

Amos was busy leading the flock.

Nehemiah was busy as the king's cupbearer.

Peter and Andrew were busy casting a net into the sea.

James and John were busy mending their nets.

Matthew was collecting customs.

Saul was busy persecuting the friends of Jesus.

William Carey was busy mending and making shoes.

—*Hints and Helps*

248. OVERCOMING EVIL

"Overcome evil with good." *Rom. 12:21*

Three methods:

I. The Natural Method
   1. To overcome evil with evil
   2. "An eye for an eye, and a tooth for a tooth."

I. The Neutral Method
   1. Do nothing about it.
   2. Ignore it; pretend it doesn't exist.
   3. Endure it.

III. The Christian Method
   1. Text
   2. Illustration: Peter severs Malchus' ear; Jesus heals it.
   3. An unnatural method, but supernatural power is given.

—Adapted from an old tract, by C. H. P.

249. THE DEEP THINGS OF GOD

"God hath revealed them unto us by His Spirit: for the Spirit searcheth all things, yea, the deep things of God." *I Cor. 2:10*

The Spirit reveals to us:
1. The depths of God's love
2. The depths of God's mercy
3. The depths of God's righteousness
4. The depths of God's wisdom

—A. G. Brown

250. WORKERS WITH GOD

"We are labourers together with God." *I Cor. 3:9*

Man labors with God:

I. In Continuing the Creation
   1. God has created the world, but he depends upon man's help in subduing it.
   2. Man is told to have dominion over the world.

II. In Developing His Own Christian Character and Personality
   1. God desires to develop man into a noble and useful vessel, but man must cooperate.
   2. Our part is to be willing and obedient.

III. In Reconciling the World to God
   1. We bring the world to Christ by taking Christ to the world.
   2. We are not responsible for results, but efforts.

251. "YE ARE CHRIST'S"

"Ye are Christ's; and Christ is God's." *I Cor. 3:23*

I. By Right of Purchase
   1. "Ye are not your own. . . . Ye are bought with a price."
   2. The meaning of redemption

II. By Right of Our Dedication
   1. We have consecrated ourselves to him.
   2. Voluntary, but binding

III. By Relation
   1. We have been adopted into the family of God.
   2. We bear the name "Christian."

252. FOOLS FOR CHRIST'S SAKE

"We are fools for Christ's sake." *I Cor. 4:10*

I. Judged by the Standards of the World, Paul Was a Fool.
   1. Gave up a career as a distinguished rabbi, Pharisee, member of Sanhedrin, for Christ's sake.
   2. Endured indignities, hardships, beatings, stonings, mockery, poverty, martyrdom.

II. Thousands Have Been Willing to Be Considered Fools for Christ's Sake.
   1. Disciples; martyrs; missionaries; ministers, faithful laymen
   2. Huss, Knox, Latimer, Livingstone, Grenfel, Schweitzer
   3. Many zealous Christians branded as fools, fanatics

III. THE CHRISTIAN'S WISDOM WILL BE REVEALED IN THE LIFE TO COME.
1. The Christian has "long-range" plans.
2. When the rains descend, and the floods come, and the winds blow, it will be seen who were wise and who were foolish.

---

253. WATCH YOUR STEP

"Let him that thinketh he standeth take heed lest he fall."
I Cor. 10:12

I. ABRAHAM, FATHER OF THE FAITHFUL.
(Lied to escape embarrassment.)
II. JACOB, FOUNDER OF ISRAEL
(Took advantage of his brother's hunger to drive a sharp bargain.)
III. MOSES, THE LAWGIVER
(Slew an Egyptian.)
IV. DAVID, SWEET SINGER, LOVER OF GOD
(Character was sullied by an illicit romance.)
V. PETER, STALWART DISCIPLE, SURE OF HIMSELF
(Denied his Lord with an oath.)
VI. ALL THE DISCIPLES PLEDGED FAITHFULNESS.
("They all forsook him, and fled.")

Application: "Watch and pray."

---

254. A WORD OF PRAISE

"Now I praise you, brethren."
I Cor. 11:2

I. PRAISE IS A DUTY.
1. Conscience sanctions a word of praise.
2. Praise encourages efforts to do good.
3. Praise helps us to win others.
4. Praise discourages selfishness.

II. PRAISE IS A DIFFICULT DUTY
1. The self-centered find it all but impossible.
2. The jealous cannot praise.
3. The unsympathetic find it difficult to praise.
4. The narrow-minded seldom praise.

III. PRAISE IS A MUCH-NEGLECTED DUTY.
1. Neglected by the church.
2. Neglected in the home.
3. Neglected in social and public life

IV. PRAISE IS A DUTY REQUIRING DISCRIMINATION.

V. PRAISE IS A DUTY WHICH TESTS CHARACTER.
1. It tests your own character.
2. It tests the character of those praised.

—Dinsdale T. Young

---

255. SELF-EXAMINATION

"Let a man examine himself."
I Cor. 11:28

Just as it is wise to go to a physician for an occasional physical check-up, so it is wise to go to the Great Physician for a spiritual examination. The Holy Communion service is an excellent occasion for self-examination, introspection, with the aid of the Spirit of God.

I. WE MUST EXAMINE OUR HEARTS FOR TRACES OF SIN.
1. Sin is an insidious poison—soon gets out of control.
2. We must not treat it lightly. "Fools make a mock at sin."

II. WE NEED TO EXAMINE OUR ATTITUDES.
1. Are we in love and charity with our associates?
2. Do we love God with singleness of heart?
3. Have we the spirit of forgiveness as taught by Jesus?
4. "If any man have not the Spirit of Christ, he is none of his."

III. We Need to Re-examine Our Christian Principles, Standards, and Convictions.
1. Grave danger that contacts with the world may cause us to lower our standards.
2. Easy to drift from our moorings
3. There are many "religious has-beens."

Application: Examine self; face the facts honestly; and do something about your findings.

256. THE SPICE OF LIFE

"Now there are diversities of gifts, but the same Spirit. And there are differences of administrations, but the same Lord. And there are diversities of operations, but it is the same God which worketh all in all." *I Cor. 12:4-6*

"Variety's the very spice of life,
That gives it all its flavour."
—Cowper

The Christian religion abounds in variety. Not dull, monotonous.

I. Varieties of Christian Experience
1. Some have dramatic conversions, as Saul of Tarsus.
2. Some enter the Kingdom as little children.
3. Some make a decision from logic—Ethiopian eunuch.
4. Curiosity brings some to Christ—Zacchaeus.
5. It took an earthquake to bring the Philippian jailor to repentance.

II. Varieties in Christian Personalities
1. Apostles—no two alike
2. Shakespeare: "All the world's a stage," etc.

III. Variety in Forms of Service
1. Eph. 4:11: "Apostles: . . . prophets; . . . evangelists; . . . pastors and teachers; for the. . . ."
2. A place and a task for all who are willing

257. NOW AND THEN

"Now we see through a glass, darkly; but then face to face: now I know in part, but then shall I know even as also I am known." *I Cor. 13:12*

In our daily conversations we frequently use the phrase "now and then." The same phrase was used by Paul. Text.

In this text we have the "now" contrasted with the "then."

I. Now Our Vision Is Defective: Then It Will Be Clear.
1. *Now* many can't see through the dark clouds of sorrow, trouble, ignorance; *then* we'll understand.
2. Paul: "I reckon that the sufferings of this present time are not worthy to be compared with the glory which shall be revealed."

II. Now Our Bodies Are Subject to Change and Decay: Then Incorruptible.
1. "This corruptible must put on incorruption, and this mortal must put on immortality."
2. "Death is swallowed up in victory."

III. Now Sadness and Trouble May Be Our Lot: Then We Shall Have Joy Untold.
1. "Weeping may endure for a night [now], but joy cometh in the morning [then]."
2. God shall wipe away all tears."

IV. Now Sin Deals Woe and Death: Then We Shall Have Happiness and Life Eternal.

258. FAITH, HOPE, LOVE

"And now abideth faith, hope,

love, these three; and the greatest of these is love."

I Cor. 13:13 (A.S.V.)

1. Faith makes all things possible.
2. Hope makes all things bright.
3. Love makes all things easy.

259. ORGANIZE YOURSELF

"Let all things be done decently and in order." *I Cor. 14:40*

Many lives are lived haphazardly, without rhyme, reason, plan, or purpose. There is so much to be done, and so little time in which to do it, that we need to do it "decently and in order."

The text may be an appeal to:

1. Intelligent use of our time
2. Good housekeeping
3. Business affairs
4. Church management
5. Personal religious living

260. THE GOSPEL IN AN EPISTLE

"Moreover, brethren, I declare unto you the gospel which I preached unto you." *I Cor. 15:1*

I. The Actual Death of Christ ("Christ died." Verse 3.)

II. The Necessary Death of Christ ("Christ died for . . . sins." Verse 3.)

III. The Substitutionary Death of Christ ("Christ died for *our* sins." Verse 3.)

IV. The Prophetic Death of Christ ("Christ died . . . according to the scriptures." Verse 3.)

V. The Victorious Death of Christ ("Rose again the third day." Verse 4.)

261. PROGRESSIVE HUMILITY

"By the grace of God I am what I am." *I Cor. 15:10*

I. "Breathing Out Threatenings and Slaughter." Acts 9:1.
(Probable date A.D. 34)

II. "An Apostle." Gal. 1:1.
(Probable date A.D. 58)

III. "I Am the Least of the Apostles." I Cor. 15:9.
(Probable date A.D. 59)

IV. "Who Am Less than the Least of All Saints." Eph. 3:8.

V. "Christ Jesus Came into the World to Save Sinners; of Whom I Am Chief." I Tim. 1:15.
(Probable date A.D. 65)

VI. "The Lord Shall Deliver Me . . . , to Whom Be Glory for Ever and Ever." II Tim. 4:18.
(Probable date A.D. 66)

262. "IF CHRIST BE NOT RISEN"

"If Christ be not risen, then is our preaching vain, and your faith is also vain." *I Cor. 15:14.*

Read I Cor. 15:14-19.

If Christ be not risen, then:

1. Preaching is vain (verse 14).
2. Faith is vain (verse 14).
3. Christians are false witnesses (verse 15).
4. We are still in our sins (verse 17).
5. They who have fallen asleep have perished (verse 18).
6. "We are of all men most miserable" (verse 19).

263. VICTORY

"Thanks be to God, which giveth us the victory through our Lord Jesus Christ." *I Cor. 15:57*

Victory over:

1. The world
2. The flesh
3. The devil

264. MANHOOD AT ITS BEST

"Quit you like men, be strong."

I Cor. 16:13

I. FOR YEARS THE ATHLETIC MAN WAS THE IDEAL.
  1. The Spartans
  2. Olympic and Isthmian games
II. FOR YEARS THE ASCETIC MAN WAS THE IDEAL.
III. FOR YEARS THE PATRIOT WAS THE IDEAL MAN.
IV. FOR YEARS THE INTELLECTUAL MAN WAS THE IDEAL.
  1. Plato
  2. Socrates
  3. Homer
V. FOR YEARS THE CIVIC MAN WAS THE IDEAL.
  1. Romans boasting of their citizenship
  2. Today's "superpatriots"
VI. FOR YEARS THE JUDAIC MAN WAS THE IDEAL.
  1. Ceremonials, circumcisions, washings, etc.
  2. Pharisaism
VII. THE WORLD IS COMING TO SEE THAT THE TRUE CHRISTIAN IS THE IDEAL MAN.

—J. Ossian Davies

265. THE EFFECTS OF FAITH

"By faith ye stand."
II Cor. 1:24

1. Faith causes us to bow down before God.
2. Faith makes us stand erect before men.
3. Faith makes us stand firm against sin.

—Alexander Maclaren

266. THE DEVIL'S TRICKS

"We are not ignorant of his devices." *II Cor. 2:11*

Satan is ever alert to new ways and means to drag souls down to perdition, but he has used some of his tricks so often that intelligent people should be able to see through them.

I. HE MAKES HIMSELF ATTRACTIVE.
  1. Not the hideous personality the artists paint
  2. Paul: "Satan himself is transformed into an angel of light."
  3. "The devil is God's ape."
II. HE MAKES SIN ATTRACTIVE.
  1. Liquor advertising
  2. Tobacco commercials
III. HE GOES TO CHURCH.
  1. Job: "The sons of God came to present themselves before the Lord, and Satan came also among them."
  2. Has been known to attend the official board and ladies' aid meetings.
IV. HE URGES PROCRASTINATION
  1. He never suggests that Christians abandon religion, but urges postponement of duties, etc.
  2. He never urges a prospect to say "no" to the evangelistic appeal; just wait for a more opportune time.

267. LIVING EPISTLES

"Ye are our epistle written in our hearts, known and read of all men." *II Cor. 3:2*

I. THERE ARE MULTITUDES OF SPIRITUAL ILLITERATES.
  1. They do not read God's printed Word.
  2. Ignore the preachers.
II. BUT THEY READ CHRISTIANS.
  1. Living epistles
  2. "Disciples were called Christians. . . ."
III. WE MUST TAKE HEED THAT OUR LIVES DO NOT MISREPRESENT CHRIST.

268. THE GLORIOUS GOSPEL

"The light of the glorious gospel of Christ. . . ." *II Cor. 4:4*

The Christian gospel is:

1. Glorious in its doctrines (John 3:16; Luke 4:18).
2. Glorious in its provisions (I Tim. 2:4-6; Rom. 5:18-19).

3. Glorious in the prospects it reveals (Mic. 4:2-4; Rev. 7:16-17).

269. HOW TO PREACH

"We preach not ourselves, but Christ Jesus the Lord."
II Cor. 4:5

1. The gospel is a fact; therefore tell it simply.
2. It is a joyful fact; therefore tell it cheerfully.
3. It is an entrusted fact; therefore tell it faithfully.
4. It is a fact of infinite moment; therefore tell it earnestly.
5. It is a fact of infinite love; therefore tell it pathetically.
6. It is a fact difficult of comprehension; therefore tell it with illustration.
7. It is a fact about a person; therefore preach Christ.

270. THE COURAGE OF CONVICTION

"As it is written, I believed, and therefore have I spoken; we also believe, and therefore speak."
II Cor. 4:13

Paul is quoting David and appropriating his sentiments. Paul had the courage to speak his convictions, regardless of consequences.

Certain other Bible characters were noted for the courage to stand by their convictions:

I. Joseph Versus Potiphar's Wife
   1. Preferred prison to an immoral act.
   2. Glamour and glitter do not justify sin.

II. Daniel Versus Nebuchadnezzar
   1. Spurned the king's wine and dainties.
   2. Later, preferred the lion's den to a prayerless home.

III. John the Baptist Versus Herod
   1. Told him what he thought, even though it meant prison and death.
   2. Luther: "Here I stand."

IV. Disciples Versus a Mocking World
   1. Went everywhere, preaching the word.
   2. The world has mistreated God's prophets.

V. Jesus Versus Satan
   1. Tempted in the wilderness; sturdily resisted.
   2. Set his face to go up to Jerusalem, even though it meant crucifixion.

271. THE REALITY OF THE UNSEEN

"We look not at the things which are seen, but at the things which are not seen: for the things which are seen are temporal; but the things which are not seen are eternal."
II Cor. 4:18

I. Many Attach No Value to Things the Eye Cannot See or the Hands Touch.
   1. "Having eyes, see ye not?"
   2. Thomas: "Except I shall see in his hands the print of the nails, and put my finger into the print . . . , I will not believe."
   3. "Man shall not live by bread alone." He needs spiritual food as well.
   4. We recognize the reality of some things that cannot be seen: pain, odor, wind, cold, heat.
   5. The Spirit of God is real.

II. We Need to Recognize the Importance of the Unseen.
   1. Elisha and Gehazi
   2. "We . . . are compassed about. . . ."
   3. Zechariah: "Not by might, nor by power, but. . . ."
   4. Stephen: "I see the heavens opened, and the Son of man. . . ." Others couldn't see this.

Application:

All need to pray: "Open thou mine eyes."

Matthew Henry: "None so blind as those that will not see."

272. CHRISTIANITY CHANGES THINGS

"If any man be in Christ, he is a new creature: old things are passed away; behold, all things are become new." *II Cor. 5:17*

Christianity changes:

I. A Man's Existence into a Life
  1. "I am come that they might have life, and . . . have it more abundantly."
  2. "I live, yet not I, but Christ liveth in me."
  3. "Beauty for ashes"

II. A House into a Home
  1. "A lot of houses ought to be remodeled into homes."
  2. Homes are happiest where Christ is the "Head of the house."
  3. The transformation in Zacchaeus' home

III. A Jungle into a Civilization
  1. "The wilderness and the solitary place shall be glad for them; and the desert shall rejoice, and blossom as the rose."

IV. The Rule of Gold into the Golden Rule

V. Swords into Plowshares
  1. Hate and carnage must give way to peace and good will.

Application: Christianity puts heaven into us before we get into heaven.

273. WORKERS TOGETHER

"We then, as workers together with him, beseech you also that ye receive not the grace of God in vain." *II Cor. 6:1*

I. To Build Up the Church Requires Work, and Lots of It.
  1. This is true of a garden, farm, business, education, anything worth while.
  2. When you see a strong church, you may safely assume somebody has been laboring to make it so.

II. Christian Work Should Be Co-operative.
  1. Co-operation needed in business, family, militarism, civic life, athletics
  2. Mechanical things: clock; engine; locomotives
  3. We as Christians are "workers together."

III. We Must Work Under Divine Direction—"With Him."
  1. Some accept Jesus as Saviour, but not as Lord and Master.
  2. "Why call ye me, Lord, Lord, and do not the . . . ?"

Application: We must work; work together; with Christ.

274. THE LIBERAL MACEDONIANS

"First [they] gave their own selves to the Lord." *II Cor. 8:5*

I. Profusely Liberal
  ("Beyond their power"—verse 3)

II. Purely Voluntary
  ("They were willing of themselves"—verse 3.)

III. To One They Could Trust
  (Appointed Paul administrator.)

IV. The Secret of Their Liberality
  (They had already given themselves to the Lord.)

275. RICHES THROUGH POVERTY

"For ye know the grace of our Lord Jesus Christ, that, though he was rich, yet for your sakes he became poor, that ye through his poverty might be rich." *II Cor. 8:9*

I. Christ Was Rich.
  1. In material possessions. Co-Creator of the world:

"All things were made by him; and. . . ." "The earth is the Lord's, and. . . ." "The cattle upon a thousand hills" are his.
2. In the love and affection of the Father
3. In glory and honor

II. Christ Divested Himself of His Wealth.
1. "Made himself of no reputation, and took upon him the form of a servant."
2. Born in penury.
3. Raised in humble environment.
4. Became an itinerant preacher. "The foxes have holes, and the birds of the air have nests; but the Son of man hath not. . . ."
5. On the cross felt forsaken of God.

III. The Rich Christ Became Poor for Our Sakes.

Application: "We taste the sweet spices of Arabia, yet never know the scorching suns that brought them forth."

276. CHRISTIAN SIMPLICITY

". . . the simplicity that is in Christ." *II Cor. 11:3*

The most casual student of the life of Christ cannot help noting the beautiful simplicity that characterized him.

I. His Mode of Life Was Simple.
1. It puts our artificial lives to shame.
2. Our civilization too complex

II. His Teachings Were Marked by Simplicity.
1. The common people heard him gladly.
2. He drew illustrations from the commonplace.

III. The Lord's Supper Was a Simple Memorial.
1. A cup of wine and a fragment of bread were used as symbols of his broken body and shed blood.
2. Christ certainly disapproves of many innovations with this sacrament.

Application: The Christian world has need to get back to "the simplicity that is in Christ."

277. PAUL'S AFFLICTIONS

"Most gladly therefore will I rather glory in my infirmities, that the power of Christ may rest upon me." *II Cor. 12:9*

1. Infirmity (Gal. 4:13)
2. Body weak (II Cor. 10:10)
3. Weariness (II Cor. 11:27)
4. Afflictions (Col. 1:24)
5. Sufferings (II Tim. 3:10-11)
6. Despaired of life (II Cor. 1:8)
7. Body scarred (Acts 16:23, 33; II Cor. 11:25; Gal. 6:17)
8. Thorn in the flesh (II Cor. 12:7-10)
9. Poor eyesight (Gal. 6:11)

278. A PARADOX

"I take pleasure in infirmities, in reproaches, in necessities, in persecutions, in distresses for Christ's sake: for when I am weak, then am I strong." *II Cor. 12:10*

I. When Are Christians Weak? When They Think They Are Strong.
1. Samson "wist not that the Lord was departed."
2. Peter boasted of his strength; denied his Lord.
3. It has been said that a man isn't really educated until he is appalled at his own ignorance; and no man is strong who doesn't realize his weakness.

II. When Are Christians Strong? When They Realize Their Weakness.
1. Text
2. Paul: "I can do all things

through Christ which strengtheneth me."
3. Jesus told Paul: "My strength is made perfect in weakness."

Application: "Be strong in the Lord."

279. WHAT IS CHRISTIAN ZEAL?

"It is good to be zealously affected always in a good thing." *Gal. 4:18*

What is true Christian zeal?

1. Not mere noise and excitement.
2. Not a contest for creeds and forms.
3. Not unchristianizing those who do not utter our "shibboleth."
4. It is a burning desire for God's glory and the good of men.
5. It is a spirit of self-sacrifice for Christ.

—William W. Wythe

280. LIKE BEGETS LIKE

"Whatsoever a man soweth, that shall he also reap." *Gal. 6:7*

1. A man expects to reap that which he sows.
2. He expects to reap more than he sows.
3. Ignorance of the kind of seed sown will make no difference to the crop.

—Dwight L. Moody

281. DON'T QUIT

"Let us not be weary in well doing: for in due season we shall reap, if we faint not." *Gal. 6:9*

Why do Christians become weary in welldoing?

1. Sometimes they have a secret desire for ease.
2. Sometimes they rebel at the self-denials and sacrifices involved.
3. Occasionally they have false humility.
4. The feeling that fellow Christians are not doing their share of the work.
5. Always, Satan employs the "slow-up" technique to accomplish his ends.

282. THE OLD RUGGED CROSS

"God forbid that I should glory, save in the cross of our Lord Jesus Christ." *Gal. 6:14*

We cherish the cross because:

I. OUR REDEMPTION IS THROUGH THE BLOOD SHED UPON IT.
1. "Peace through the blood of his cross." Col. 1:20.
2. "Redeemed . . . with the precious blood of Christ"

II. IT IS THE SYMBOL OF CHRIST'S SACRIFICIAL LOVE.
1. "He . . . became obedient unto death, even the death of the cross." Phil. 2:8.
2. "Greater love hath no man than this."

III. IT IS THE STANDARD UNDER WHICH COMPLETE VICTORY OVER SIN AND THE WORLD IS TO BE WON.
1. "In this sign conquer."
2. "Onward, Christian soldiers,
. . . .
With the cross of Jesus
Going on before."

IV. IT IS LUMINOUS AND THROWS LIGHT ON THE UNKNOWN FUTURE.
1. "All the light of sacred story
Gathers round its head sublime."
2. "God forbid that I should glory, save in the cross of our Lord Jesus Christ."

283. A GODLESS WORLD

"Having no hope, and without God in the world." *Eph. 2:12*

I. SUPPOSE GOD SHOULD WITHDRAW FROM THE MATERIAL UNIVERSE!
1. "Without form, and void; and darkness . . ."
2. No law of gravitation
3. No cycling seasons

4. No rain, sunshine, flowers, animal life

II. SUPPOSE HE SHOULD WITHDRAW FROM THE MORAL UNIVERSE!
1. No Christian people; churches; ideals; restraints
2. No Christian principles in industry
3. No Sabbaths; no religious music, art, literature

III. THINK WHAT IT WOULD MEAN TO THE HOME.

IV. THINK WHAT IT WOULD MEAN TO THE NATION.
1. "The wicked shall be turned into hell, and all the nations that forget God."
2. History verifies this prediction.

V. WHAT WOULD IT MEAN TO YOU PERSONALLY?
1. No hope of immortality; no comfort in sorrow; no philosophy of suffering; no anchor for faith; nothing to look forward to
2. No reunion with dear ones after death

284. CITIZENS OF HEAVEN

"Now therefore ye are no more strangers and foreigners, but fellowcitizens with the saints, and of the household of God."
Eph. 2:19

This text means that we:

I. ARE UNDER HEAVEN'S GOVERNMENT.
(Christ, the King of heaven, rules and reigns in our hearts.)

II. SHARE THE HONORS OF HEAVEN.
(The glory of the saints; the spotless robe; the honors of citizenship.)

III. HAVE ANGELS AND SAINTS FOR OUR COMPANIONS.

IV. HAVE COMMON RIGHTS TO ALL ITS PROPERTY.

V. MAY ENJOY ITS IMMORTAL DELIGHTS.

—Charles H. Spurgeon

285. THE MEASURELESS LOVE OF CHRIST

". . . that ye may be able to comprehend with all saints what is the breadth, and length, and depth, and height; and to know the love of Christ, which passeth knowledge."
Eph. 3:18-19

The love of Christ cannot be measured; it has no limits; it is like a shoreless ocean whose depths have not been sounded.

The love of Christ may be said to be directional:

I. IT HAS BREADTH.
1. It is broad enough to embrace all mankind; it encircles the globe, includes all colors and castes, rich and poor, high and low.
2. "The love of God is broader than the measure of man's mind."

II. IT HAS LENGTH.
1. It is as long as eternity.
2. "I have loved thee with an everlasting love."

III. IT HAS DEPTH.
1. It is deep enough to reach down from heaven to the deepest abyss of sin. "He brought me up . . . out of an horrible pit."
2. No sinner so depraved, no prodigal sunken so low, that Christ's love cannot reach down to him.

IV. IT HAS HEIGHT.
1. So high it overshadows all human loves.
2. "Love divine, all loves excelling."

286. HE IS ABLE

"[He] is able to do exceeding abundantly above all that we ask or think."
Eph. 3:20

He is able to do:

1. "All that we ask"
2. "All that we ask or think"
3. "Above all that we ask or think"

4. "Abundantly above all that we ask or think"

5. "Exceeding abundantly above all that we ask or think"

Application:

1. He is not only able, but willing.

2. Yet he cannot impart his blessings to us without our willingness to accept.

287. HONESTY, INDUSTRY, CHARITY

"Let him that stole steal no more: but rather let him labour, working with his hands the thing which is good, that he may have to give to him that needeth."
Eph. 4:28

1. "Let him that stole steal no more"—that's honesty.

2. "Let him labour, working with his hands"—that's industry.

3. "That he may have to give to him that needeth"—that's charity.

288. THE SOCIABILITY OF SIN

"Be not ye therefore partakers with them." *Eph. 5:7*

We partake of the sins of others:
1. When we practice their sins
2. When we concur with them
3. When we prompt them to sin
4. When we impose no restraints upon them

—Clarkson

289. SNAP OUT OF IT!

"Awake thou that sleepest, and arise from the dead, and Christ shall give thee light." *Eph. 5:14*

1. What is the sinner's state? Asleep.

2. How did he become so? Relaxation; semiconsciousness; sound slumber.

3. How is he kept so? The devil rocks his cradle.

4. How may his state be described? As dreaming.

5. Will he ever awake? Yes, either through conviction or condemnation.

6. What is the gospel call? Text.

—Miller

290. WHAT IS THE CHURCH?

"Christ . . . loved the church, and gave himself for it."
Eph. 5:25

The church is:
1. The perpetuation of the life of Christ on earth
2. "The pillar of truth"
3. The promotor of ideals
4. The preacher of service

—O. F. Blackwelder

291. WHAT IS YOUR MOTIVE?

"For this is right." *Eph. 6:1*

I. MOTIVE, THE SPRING OF ALL HUMAN ACTION
   1. Good
   2. Bad
   3. Mixed

II. MOTIVES THAT ARE UNWORTHY
   1. It is pleasant.
   2. It is popular.
   3. It is profitable.

III. THE ONE TRUE MOTIVE
   1. Text: "This is right."

—W. W. Wythe

292. TO DIE IS GAIN

"To me to live is Christ, and to die is gain." *Phil. 1:21*

This is true of the Christian:
1. Physically
2. Mentally
3. Morally
4. Socially
5. Eternally

—Payne

293. CHRISTIAN CONVERSATION

"Let your conversation be as it becometh the gospel of Christ."
Phil. 1:27

The Christian's conversation should be marked by:
1. Simplicity

2. Truth
3. Candor
4. Gentleness
5. Love
6. Holiness unto the Lord

294. THE MIND OF CHRIST

"Let this mind be in you, which was also in Christ Jesus."
Phil. 2:5

Read Phil. 2:5-11.
The mind of Christ toward:
1. God
2. Man
3. Death
4. Glory

295. HUMBLED AND EXALTED

"He humbled himself, and became obedient unto death, even the death of the cross. Wherefore God also hath highly exalted him, and given him a name which is above every name." *Phil. 2:8-9*

Read Phil. 2:7-11.

I. HIS HUMILIATION
   1. He made himself of no reputation.
   2. He took upon him the form of a servant.
   3. Made in the likeness of men
   4. Found in fashion as a man
   5. He humbled himself.
   6. Obedient unto death
   7. Even the death of the cross

II. HIS EXALTATION
   1. Exalted by God
   2. A name above every name
   3. At his name every knee should bow.
   4. Of things in heaven
   5. Of things on earth
   6. Things under the earth
   7. And every tongue confess that Jesus is Lord.

296. IN HIS NAME

"God also hath highly exalted him, and given him a name which is above every name." *Phil. 2:9*

I. SURRENDERING
(For his name's sake—Matt. 19:29)

II. SEPARATION
(Gathered in his name—Matt. 18:20)

III. SUFFERING
(Hated for his name's sake—Matt. 10:22)

IV. SERVING
(Working in his name—Mark 9:41)

V. SUPPLICATION
(Praying in his name—John 14:13)

VI. STRENGTH
(Holding fast in his name—Rev. 2:13)

297. MAJORING IN MINORS

"This one thing I do."
Phil. 3:13

Two words pretty well tell the story of Paul's greatness—consecration and concentration.

I. PAUL MAJORED IN THE WILL OF GOD.
   1. Truly could he say: "Thy will; nothing more; nothing else; nothing less."
   2. Christ's will had a "priority rating" with him.

II. MANY MODERN CHURCHMEN ARE "MAJORING IN MINORS."
   1. Put second things in first place.
   2. "Too many petty causes get too much loyalty."
   3. Isaiah: "Wherefore . . . spend money for that which is not bread, and your labour for that which satisfieth not?"

III. HOW ABOUT OURSELVES?
   1. What has pre-eminence in our lives?
   2. Can we say, "This one thing I do"? Or is it, "These forty things I dabble in"?

298. POWER UNLIMITED

"I can do all things through

Christ which strengthetheneth me."
Phil. 4:13

The Philippians seem to have had an inferiority complex when it came to undertaking the larger things for Christ and the Church, and Paul sought to give them courage.

I. "I Can Do All Things."
  1. Not the words of a braggart, but those of a man who has discovered what God can do through a consecrated Christian.
  2. "In the lexicon of youth there is no such word as fail." This may also be said of the lexicon of the Christian.
  3. It is a false modesty, an irreligious humility, to discount what the Lord can do through you.

II. "I Can Do All Things."
  1. "All things" that are within the will and purposes of God.
  2. The church has always specialized in doing the seemingly impossible.

III. "Through Christ Which Strengtheneth Me."
  1. This relieves Paul of any stigma of egotism.
  2. When the Lord orders something done, he gives the power to accomplish it.
  3. "Not by might, nor by power, but by my spirit, saith the Lord of hosts" (Zech. 4:6).

299. THE IDEAL CHRISTIAN

"We . . . do not cease to pray for you, and to desire that ye might be filled with the knowledge of his will in all wisdom and spiritual understanding." *Col. 1:9*

Read Col. 1:9-13.

1. "Filled with the knowledge of his will" (verse 9)
2. "Walk worthy." (verse 10)
3. "Fruitful in every good work" (verse 10)
4. Growth: "increasing in the knowledge of God" (verse 10)
5. Power: "Strengthened . . ." (verse 11)
6. Grace of gratitude (verse 12)
7. Deliverance from darkness (verse 13)
8. Translated (verse 13)

300. THE RISEN LIFE

"If ye then be risen with Christ, seek those things which are above."
Col. 3:1

I. An Appeal to Christians to Act like Christians.
  1. The Christian is a citizen of two worlds. His feet are on the ground, his head above the clouds.
  2. The true Christian lives a new life, on a higher level. Affections are on things above.

II. "If Risen, . . . Seek. . . ."
  1. Life's higher values must be sought.
  2. The "things above" are attained by climbing.

III. If We Are Risen with Christ, We Must Rise Above:
  1. Our humanity. Paul: "I keep under my body."
  2. Worldly standards of right and wrong.
  3. Questionable amusements and pleasures.
  4. Things mean, petty, childish.

IV. What Are "Those Things above" We Are to Seek?
  1. Answer is in Phil. 4:8: "Whatsoever things are true, . . . honest, . . . pure, . . . lovely," etc.

V. The Master's Promise.
  1. "Seek, and ye shall find."
  2. "Blessed are they which do hunger and thirst after righteousness: for they shall be filled."

301. YOUR SPIRITUAL WARDROBE

"Above all these things put on love, which is the bond of perfectness." *Col. 3:14* (*A.S.V.*)

Clothing styles come and go. Every season brings its changes. But in the realm of the spirit there are some garments that never fade, never wear out, never go out of style.

Paul mentions some of these garments in Col. 3:12-14.

I. "Put on Compassion." (Verse 12.)
   1. A Christian without compassion is something else—and less—than Christian.
   2. "Rejoice with them that do rejoice, and weep with them that weep."

II. "Put on Kindness." (Verse 12.)
   1. "Kindness is compassion in action."
   2. The Priest and the Levite probably had compassion, of a sort, but the Samaritan was both compassionate and kind.

III. "Put on Humbleness of Mind, Meekness." (Verse 12.)
   1. Pet. 5:5: "Be clothed with humility."
   2. "Blessed are the meek."

IV. "Put on Forbearance, Forgiveness." (Verse 13.)

V. "Put on Love." (Verse 14.)
   1. "Above all"—the most important garment
   2. The mark of a Christian

Application: Have you checked your spiritual wardrobe lately?

302. SILENCE!

"Study to be quiet."
I Thess. 4:11

I. Quietness, or Silence, Is Not a Void, or an Absence of Something.
   1. In the sense that darkness is an absence of light
   2. Silence is a positive quality.

II. The Supreme Value Quietude Brings to Us Is an Awareness of the Presence of God.
   1. "Be still, and know that I am God."
   2. "God's voice is not heard in a crowd."
   3. "Come ye yourselves apart. . . ."

III. "Study" to Be Quiet.
   1. The day's schedule must be planned so as to include a period of silence, meditation, quietness.
   2. "Be still, my soul."
   3. Moses had to "turn aside" before God spoke out of the burning bush.

303. HOLD FAST

"Hold fast that which is good."
I Thess. 5:21

Hold fast:

1. "The form of sound words" (II Tim. 1:13)
2. "The faithful word" (Tit. 1:9)
3. "Confidence and . . . hope" (Heb. 3:6)
4. "Our profession" (Heb. 4:14)
5. "Thy crown" (Rev. 3:11)

304. UNREASONABLE MEN

"Pray for us, . . . that we may be delivered from unreasonable . . . men." *II Thess. 3:1, 2*

Paul asked the Thessalonian church folks to pray for his deliverance from unreasonable men —presumably churchmen—who were adding to his burdens.

In every generation there have been unreasonable churchmen who have made life difficult for preachers:

1. Men who want a ministerial mouthpiece

2. Men who expect ministerial perfection
3. Men who desire a ministerial drudge
4. Men who allow a ministerial pauper
5. Men who wish a ministerial proxy

305. HISTORY IS HIS STORY

"This is a faithful saying, and worthy of all acceptation, that Christ Jesus came into the world to save sinners." *I Tim. 1:15*

1. The coming of Christ into the world is the chief fact in its history.
2. Opposition to Christianity is the greatest sin in the world's history.
3. The pardon of sin is the chief display of mercy in the world's history.
4. These facts demand the attention of man above all other facts of history.

—Morris

306. PRAYER-MEETING BENEFITS

"I exhort . . . that, first of all, supplications, prayers, intercessions, and giving of thanks, be made for all men." *I Tim. 2:1*

Some benefits:

1. Soul rest and refreshment (Mark 6:31).
2. Mutual encouragement (Heb. 10:25).
3. Spiritual edification (I Cor. 14:26).
4. Increase of faith (John 20: 26-29).
5. Conversion of unbelievers (I Cor. 14:24-25).
6. Helpfulness to the pastor (Eph. 6:18-19).
7. Christ's promised presence (Matt. 18:19-20).
8. Spiritual joy and gladness (Col. 3:16).

307. WHAT'S RIGHT WITH THE CHURCH

". . . the church of the living God, the pillar and ground of the truth." *I Tim. 3:15*

I. Christ Is the "Chief Cornerstone."
II. The Church Still Stands for "Holiness unto the Lord."
III. The Church Has a Generous Heart.
IV. The Church Is "the Salt of the Earth."
V. The Church Is the Custodian of "the Good News."
VI. The Church Is the Vestibule of Heaven.

308. IT'S A MYSTERY TO ME

"Great is the mystery of godliness." *I Tim. 3:16*

I. Great Is the Mystery of Regeneration.
1. How God can lift men from "the miry pit," snatch them as "brands from the burning," and transform them into noble and devoted Christian leaders is a mystery—but clearly in evidence.
2. "Marvel not . . . , ye must be born again."

II. Great Is the Mystery of the Atonement.
1. How God can transform a hated cross into a precious symbol of love is a mystery.
2. "His ways [are] past finding out!"
3. We are not saved by understanding theology, but by faith in Christ.

III. Great Is the Mystery of Prayer.

"I know not by what methods rare,
But this I know, God answers prayer."
—Whittier

"More things are wrought by prayer

Than this world dreams of."
—Tennyson

309. SPIRITUAL EXERCISE

"Exercise thyself . . . unto godliness." *I Tim. 4:7*

All recognize the value and necessity of physical exercise to physical growth, strength, efficiency, and life itself.

This is no less true of the spirit. Our spiritual lives need exercise.

I. WE MUST EXERCISE OUR HANDS.
   1. "Whatsoever thy hand findeth to do, do it with thy might."
   2. "There are burdens to be lifted, cups of water to be given, broken bodies to be healed, flowers to be twined into garlands for the sick, loving service to be rendered.
   3. Handclasps of friendship and welcome: "Be not forgetful to entertain strangers. . . ."

II. WE MUST EXERCISE OUR FEET.
   1. "Go ye. . . ."
   2. "How beautiful . . . the feet of him that bringeth good tidings."
   3. All Christians are on the "go-out committee."

III. WE MUST EXERCISE OUR LIPS.
   1. Singing the songs of the church
   2. Witnessing for Christ
   3. Words of admonition; words of love; comfort

IV. WE MUST EXERCISE OUR MINDS.
   1. Read Phil. 4:8, and "think on these things."
   2. II Tim. 2:15: "Study to shew thyself approved."

310. ADVICE TO A YOUNG PREACHER

(Or any young Christian)

"Let no man despise thy youth." *I Tim. 4:12*

Read I Tim. 4:12-14.

In Bible times, as now, young people were bombarded with criticism. Paul here tells young Timothy, a ministerial student, how to command the respect of his elders.

I. "BE THOU AN EXAMPLE." (Verse 12.)
   1. By consistent, holy living, and consistent following of the teachings of Christ.
   2. Some can't be eloquent, dynamic, learned, good-looking, talented—but all can live the life.
   3. "Ye are our epistle."

II. "GIVE ATTENDANCE TO READING, TO EXHORTATION, TO DOCTRINE." (Verse 13.)
   1. Be a student as well as a saint.
   2. "Study to shew thyself approved unto God."
   3. Study doctrine.
   4. Study ways and means of increasing efficiency.

III. NEGLECT NOT THE GIFT THAT IS IN THEE." (Verse 14.)
   1. Develop talents.
   2. Neglected talents are taken from us.

311. PLAY THE GAME

"If a man . . . strive for masteries, yet is he not crowned, except he strive lawfully." *II Tim. 2:5*

The figure of speech in the text is probably influenced by the ancient athletic games, or tournaments.

Some elements of success in both athletics and religion:

I. ABIDE BY THE RULES.
   1. Athletes have their rules and codes; the Christian has his Holy Bible.
   2. "Play the game."

II. ENTHUSIASM
   1. "It is good to be zealously

affected always in a good thing." Paul.
2. The church could use some of the enthusiasm certain members have for athletics.

III. TRAINING
1. Athletic prowess comes of long training.
2. Christian efficiency does not come by chance.

IV. TEAMWORK
1. "Workers together"
2. Unity is both good and pleasant.

V. SELF-CONTROL
1. The athlete disciplines his body to make it better able to win in contests.
2. Paul said: "I keep under my body, and bring it into subjection."

312. WHAT MUST I DO TO BE USED?

"If a man therefore purge himself from these, he shall be a vessel unto honour, sanctified, and meet for the master's use. . . . Follow righteousness, faith, charity, peace, with them that call on the Lord out of a pure heart."
II Tim. 2:21-22

I. BE CLEAN. (Verse 21.)
1. In thought
2. In word
3. In actions

II. BE EARNEST. (Verse 22.)
1. In prayer
2. In Bible study
3. In concern for others

III. BE CONSECRATED. (Verses 21-22.)
1. Motives controlled by a pure heart
2. Separated from the world
3. Separated unto Christ

—A. G. Annette

313. IN THE GOOD OLD SUMMERTIME

"Be instant in season, out of season." *II Tim. 4:2*

Some "do's" and "don'ts" for Christians in the summertime:

I. SEE THE CREATOR IN HIS CREATIONS.
1. "I will lift up mine eyes unto the hills."
2. "The desert shall rejoice, and blossom as the rose."
3. "They that go down to the sea . . . these see the works of the Lord, and his wonders.
4. Joyce Kilmer's "Trees."
5. Maltbie Babcock: "This is my Father's world."

II. BE ALERT TO SUMMER TEMPTATIONS.
1. Many have a moral "letdown" in summer.
2. The Christian has no double standard—one for winter, another for summer.

III. "REMEMBER THE SABBATH DAY TO KEEP IT HOLY."
1. This was meant for summer as well as winter.
2. Text

IV. DO SOME "GROWING" IN SUMMER.
1. Increased opportunities for religious reading, meditation, prayer.
2. "Grow in grace." Peter.

Application:

"Count that day lost whose low descending sun
Views from thy hand no worthy action done."

314. LOOKING BACKWARD

"I have fought a good fight, I have kept the faith." *II Tim. 4:7*

In all the long history of Christianity there is no record of one individual, in old age, having been sorry for:

I. HAVING "FOUGHT A GOOD FIGHT."
1. For having worn the Christian's armor, and used the "sword of the Spirit"

2. For having endured "hardness, as a good soldier of Jesus Christ"

II. HAVING "FINISHED MY COURSE."

1. The race is not to the swift, nor the battle to the strong—but to the true and faithful.
2. Many start the race of life; many fall by the wayside.

III. HAVING "KEPT THE FAITH"

1. The Christian life a stewardship, and it "is required of a steward that a man be found faithful."
2. "Faithful unto death, . . . a crown of life."

315. A CHRISTIAN A.W.O.L.

"Demas hath forsaken me, having loved this present world."
II Tim. 4:10

When a soldier or sailor is "Absent Without Leave," it is a serious offense. When a Christian soldier deserts the church, it is likewise a serious matter.

The name of Demas is found three times in the writings of Paul:

I. HE IS CALLED "DEMAS, MY FELLOW-LABOURER." (Philem. 24.)

1. A complimentary term.
2. Indicates he was a worker.

II. "DEMAS" (Col. 4:14.)

1. Merely his name is mentioned. Nothing is said of his loyalty or service, although compliments are paid in context to other workers.
2. He was "just a name on the book."

III. "DEMAS HATH FORSAKEN ME." (II Tim. 4:10.)

1. Finis
2. What a tragedy!
3. And a similar tragedy occurs many times in every church.

316. BODY, MIND, SPIRIT

"The cloke that I left at Troas with Carpus, when thou comest, bring with thee, and the books, but especially the parchments."
II Tim. 4:13

Paul, a prisoner in Rome, wrote to young Timothy asking him to bring certain items he needed:

I. A CLOAK

1. He needed the cloak to keep him warm in the cold, damp, drafty prison.
2. The body has needs.

II. "BOOKS"

1. He would improve his opportunity to study. He was a student as well as a saint.
2. In modern times many prisoners, invalids, and shut-ins have improved their opportunities to get a good education.

III. "PARCHMENTS"

1. Presumably these were portions of the Scriptures.
2. The soul needs nourishment.

Application: Every Christian should be interested in:

1. The care and comfort of his body
2. The improvement of his mind
3. The deepening of his spiritual life

317. OUR SAVIOUR

"Grace, mercy, and peace, from God the Father and the Lord Jesus Christ our Saviour."
Tit. 1:4

1. Promised—in Eden (Gen. 3:15)
2. Provided—in Bethlehem (Luke 2:11)
3. Presented—at Jerusalem (Luke 2:22)
4. Preached—everywhere (Acts 5:31; Mark 16:15)

318. A PRISONER OF THE LORD

"For love's sake I rather be-

seech thee, being such an one as Paul the aged, and now also a prisoner of Jesus Christ."
Philem. 9

Just as it is considered an honor to wear the "Purple Heart," or to have been a "prisoner of war," so Paul made it clear he was proud of the scars he had received for Jesus' sake. See II Cor. 11:23-33.

How often he was in prison for Christ's sake is not clear, but in II Cor. 11:23 he mentions that it was frequently.

The three recorded instances of his imprisonment are:

I. At Philippi, A.D. 52. (See Acts 16.)
II. At Caesarea, A.D. 60. (See Acts 21 and 26.)
III. At Rome, A.D. 62-63. (See Acts 27–28.)

Application:

"Must I be carried to the skies
On flowery beds of ease,
While others fought to win the prize,
And sailed thro' bloody seas?"
—Isaac Watts

319. DRIFTING ALONG

"We ought to give the more earnest heed to the things which we have heard, lest at any time we should let them slip." *Heb. 2:1*

The drifter

I. Is Always Going Down.
1. No one drifts upgrade.
2. Law of "spiritual gravitation"
3. "Any dead fish can float downstream."

II. Is Seldom Aware He Is Drifting.
1. Samson "wist not that the Lord was departed from him."
2. Satan seldom urges a Christian to quit the church and his faith. His strategy is to urge relaxation, drifting.

III. Endangers Other Lives.
1. Derelicts endanger other ships.
2. Aimless, ambitionless spiritual drifters are often a menace to the spiritual welfare of others.

IV. Comes to Ruin at Last
1. The waters at first seem placid; then the rapids; then the falls.
2. There is a point of no return.

Application: "Rivers and men get crooked by following the line of least resistance."

320. NO ESCAPE

"How shall we escape, if we neglect so great salvation . . . ?"
Heb. 2:3

I. Consider the Great Salvation.
1. It is great in its conception—none but an infinite mind could have conceived it.
2. Great in results: freedom from sin; freedom from eternal death; promises eternal life
3. Its greatness appears in the price paid for it.

II. The Inquiry: "How Shall We Escape, If—?"
1. If those living in a darker age were punished for transgression, much more may we expect to be, who live in the present age.
2. "Unto whomsoever much is given, of him shall be much required."

Conclusion: It is not necessary that we become notoriously sinful; simply to *neglect* is to come short of this *great salvation.*
—M. R. Drury

321. THE TEMPTATIONS OF JESUS

"[He] was in all points tempted like as we are, yet without sin."
Heb. 4:15

I. Jesus Was Not Sinless in

THAT HE COULDN'T SIN.

1. Text
2. If possibility hadn't existed, his temptations would have been farcical.

II. JESUS' TEMPTATIONS WERE MANY, AND VARIED.

1. The Temptation in the Wilderness—to use his miraculous power selfishly and dramatically; to turn aside from his life's purpose
2. Other temptations might be listed:
   a. To "give a sign"—satisfy people's demand for innovations, stunts
   b. To call down fire upon the Samaritans
   c. To purge Jewry of scribes and Pharisees
   d. To use his power to release himself from Pilate's court
   e. To "come down from the cross"

III. SUPPOSE JESUS HAD YIELDED TO TEMPTATION.

1. Had he done so, he would have been an imperfect instrument for the Atonement.
2. Had he done so, he could hardly have had influence with others he was counseling to resist Satan.
3. Had he done so, the powers of hell and darkness would prevail.

Application: "Resist the devil, and he will flee from you."

322. THE BY-PRODUCTS OF SALVATION

". . . things that accompany salvation. . . ." *Heb. 6:9*

In preparing commodities for the market, producers conserve the off-falls and make of them by-products: oil, coal, wood, meat, metals, etc.

The great objective of Christianity is the salvation of the individual, but many blessings come incidentally.

I. THE BEARING OF TESTIMONY

1. If you have religion, it will express itself.
2. If a light does not shine, it isn't light.

II. THE TRANSFORMATION OF CHARACTER AND PERSONALITY

1. "If any man be in Christ, he is a new creature."
2. Illustration: the transformation of Saul of Tarsus
3. Christianity transforms a man's existence into a life, his house into a home, a jungle into a civilization, a polyglot world into a brotherhood.

III. SERENITY

1. Salvation brings a serenity, a peace, a contentment, into the hearts of men, which the world can neither give nor take away.
2. Christians can, with Paul and Silas, sing songs at midnight.

323. TO THE UTTERMOST

"He is able also to save them to the uttermost that come unto God by him, seeing he ever liveth to make intercession for them." *Heb. 7:25*

"To the uttermost." What does this mean?

I. THE UTTERMOST OF HUMAN SINS

(Whatever that uttermost sin may be)

II. THE UTTERMOST OF DESPAIR

III. THE UTTERMOST OF EVIL HABIT

(Drink, narcotics, social vices)

IV. THE UTTERMOST OF TEMPTATION

V. THE UTTERMOST OF TIME

—C. H. Spurgeon

324. THE PUBLIC WORSHIP OF GOD

". . . not forsaking the assembling of ourselves together, as the manner of some is." *Heb. 10:25*

1. God commands public worship.
2. The practice is as ancient as the church itself.
3. It is necessary for the carrying out of the Lord's work.
4. It is vital to the spiritual well-being of every soul.
5. Those who neglect the privilege of public worship on earth should not anticipate the privilege of worship in heaven.

325. TRIUMPHANT FAITH

"By [faith] the elders obtained a good report." *Heb. 11:2*

Faith triumphs over:

I. THE DREAD OF RIDICULE (Noah)
II. THE LOVE OF HOME AND COUNTRY (Abraham)
III. PATERNAL AFFECTION (Abraham's sacrifice of Isaac)
IV. THE LOVE OF WEALTH
V. THE LOVE OF POWER
VI. THE LOVE OF HONOR
VII. THE LOVE OF PLEASURE
VIII. THE DREAD OF DEATH

—C. Yale

326. THE PLEASURES OF SIN

". . . to enjoy the pleasures of sin for a season." *Heb. 11:25*

I. THERE MAY BE PLEASURES IN SIN.
   1. Otherwise few would sin.
   2. Sinful acts are often accompanied by hilarity.
II. SINFUL PLEASURES ARE MOMENTARY—"FOR A SEASON."
   1. Unreal
   2. Unsatisfying
III. THEY COST THE LOSS OF GREATER PLEASURES.
   1. "Happy is that people, whose God is the Lord."
   2. Rich Young Ruler "went away sorrowful."
IV. THE PLEASURES OF SIN END IN RUIN AND MISERY.
   1. "The wages of sin is death."
   2. Illustration: Dives and Lazarus
   3. The rich fool

327. RUNNING LIFE'S RACE

"Let us run with patience the race that is set before us." *Heb. 12:1*

In running the race of life the Christian may learn something from the athlete.

I. THE ATHLETE LAYS ASIDE UNNECESSARY ENCUMBRANCES.
   1. The runner wears few garments, carries no equipment.
   2. The Christian allows his life at times to become cluttered with worldly cares.
   3. "Too many petty causes get too much loyalty."
II. THE ATHLETE WINS NO CONTESTS WITHOUT EFFORT AND EXERTION.
   1. The Christian cannot expect to "be carried to the skies on flowery beds of ease."
   2. The best things of life do not come by chance.
III. THE ATHLETE MUST HAVE PATIENCE, ENDURANCE.
   1. Paul urges Christians: "Let us not be weary in well doing."
   2. "He that endureth to the end shall be saved." Not those who make a spectacular start and then drop by the wayside.
IV. THE ATHLETE IS INSPIRED BY THE AUDIENCE.
   1. "We also are compassed about with so great a cloud of witnesses."

2. God, the angels, our departed, are observing.

328. WHEN GOD CHASTISES

"Despise not thou the chastening of the Lord, . . . for whom the Lord loveth he chasteneth."
Heb. 12:5, 6

1. We despise the chastening of the Lord when: We murmur against it.
2. We say there is no use in it.
3. We think it dishonorable.
4. We do not earnestly seek to amend by it.

—*Biblical Illustrator*

329. PIVOT POINTS OF HEBREWS 13:20-21

"Now the God of peace, that brought again from the dead our Lord Jesus, that great shepherd of the sheep, through the blood of the everlasting covenant, make you perfect in every good work to do his will, working in you that which is wellpleasing in his sight, through Jesus Christ; to whom be glory for ever and ever. Amen."
Heb. 13:20-21

1. The proclamation of peace: "Now the God of peace"
2. The proclamation of power: "that brought again from the dead our Lord Jesus"
3. The proclamation of protection: "that great shepherd of the sheep"
4. The proclamation of penalty: "through the blood of the everlasting covenant"
5. The proclamation of perfection: "make you perfect in every good work to do his will"
6. The proclamation of pleasure: "working in you that which is wellpleasing in his sight, through Jesus Christ"
7. The proclamation of praise: "to whom be glory for ever and ever. Amen"

—Arnold Carl Westphal

330. THE GRACE OF PATIENCE

"But let patience have her perfect work, that ye may be perfect and entire, wanting nothing."
Jas. 1:4

Patience is:

1. A needed grace—"Ye have need of patience." Heb. 10:36.
2. A bestowed power—"strengthened . . . unto patience." Col. 1:2.
3. A fruitful outcome—"Bring forth fruit with patience." Luke 8:15.
4. A forming agent—"Tribulation worketh patience." Rom. 5:3.
5. A ministerial necessity—"... approving ourselves as the ministers of God, in much patience. . . ." II Cor. 6:4.
6. A communicative blessing—"patience, experience." Rom. 5:4.
7. A noble race—"Run with patience." Heb. 12:1-2.

—F. E. Marsh

331. GIFTS OF GOD

"Every good gift and every perfect gift is from above, and cometh down from the Father of lights."
Jas. 1:17

A few of Gods' gifts are:

1. Eternal life (John 10:28).
2. Rest (Matt. 11:28).
3. Peace (John 14:27).
4. Grace (Eph. 2:8).
5. All things (I Tim. 6:17).
6. Crown of life (Rev. 2:10).
7. White robe (Rev. 6:11).

—*Preacher's Tool Basket*

332. THE UPKEEP OF FAITH

"But wilt thou know, O vain man, that faith without works is dead?"
Jas. 2:20

I. THE IMPORTANCE OF FAITH CANNOT BE OVEREMPHASIZED.
   1. "Without faith it is impossible to please [God]."
   2. "By grace are ye saved through faith."

II. But "Faith Without Works Is Dead."
1. "Why call ye me, Lord, Lord, and do not the . . . ?"
2. "If ye love me, keep my commandments."
3. The barren fig tree condemned.
4. "Why stand ye here all the day idle?"

III. Jesus' Faith Manifested Itself in Works.
1. He "went about doing good."
2. "Took upon him the form of a servant."
3. "Came not to be ministered unto, but to minister."
4. "I must work the works of him that sent me."

Application: Faith without works is not only dead; it is putrid.

333. COMMUNION WITH GOD

"Draw nigh to God, and he will draw nigh to you." *Jas. 4:8*

I. How It Is Done
1. By prayer
2. By Bible study
3. By observing "the quiet hour"
4. By Sabbath observance ("in the Spirit on the Lord's Day")
5. By church worship
6. By benevolent lives

II. The Promise
1. An awareness of God's presence
2. The blessings of fellowship with God
3. "They that wait upon the Lord shall renew their strength."

334. SITTING IN JUDGMENT

"Who art thou that judgest another?" *Jas. 4:12*

I. Excellent Reasons Why We Should Not Sit in Judgment upon Others
1. We have no authority to do so.
2. We seldom know all the essential facts.
3. It is a violation of Christ's command: "Judge not."
4. It invites reprisals.
5. It is presumptuous to do so.

II. Avoiding the Habit of Censoriousness
1. Look at the faults of others through your own.
2. Look for the good in others. It is there.
3. The fact there is evil in another is not your warrant for its publication.
4. The Golden Rule

Application: "Vengeance is mine; I will repay, saith the Lord."

335. "WHAT IS YOUR LIFE?"

"What is your life? It is even a vapour, that appeareth for a little time, and then vanisheth away." *Jas. 4:14*

My life is:

1. A journey. I will live it trustingly.
2. A task. I will live it obediently.
3. A mission. I will live it helpfully.
4. A contest. I will live it earnestly.
5. A battle. I will live it courageously.

—Rutherford H. Moore

336. CAN YOU TAKE IT?

"Behold, we count them happy which endure." *Jas. 5:11*

Let us mention a few things the average Christian must learn to endure:

I. Criticism
1. "Woe unto you, when all men shall speak well of you!"
2. "Don't mind criticism: if

it is untrue, disregard it; if unfair, keep from irritation; if it is ignorant, just smile; if it is justified, learn from it."

II. DISCIPLINE
1. "Whom the Lord loveth he chasteneth."
2. Job: "When he hath tried me, I shall come forth as gold."
3. Paul: "Endure hardness, as a good soldier of Jesus Christ."
4. Jesus: "If any man will come after me, let him deny himself."

III. TEMPTATION
1. "Happy is the man that endureth temptation."
2. No sin in being tempted; the sin is in yielding.
3. "We can't prevent birds from flying over our heads, but we can prevent them from making nests in our hair."
4. Temptation makes us strong. "Each victory will help you some other to win."

337. PREVAILING PRAYER

"The effectual fervent prayer of a righteous man availeth much."
Jas. 5:16

Consider:

1. The character of those supposed to offer the prayer—"the righteous."

2. The character of the prayer itself—"effectual, fervent." (This involves sincerity, earnestness.)

3. The results of such praying—"availeth much."

—H. A. Nelson

338. A LIVELY HOPE

"[God] hath begotten us again unto a lively hope . . . , to an inheritance incorruptible, and undefiled, and that fadeth not away, reserved in heaven for you."
I Pet. 1:3-4

This hope is:
1. Death-proof—"incorruptible"
2. Dirt-proof—"undefiled"
3. Decay - proof — "reserved in heaven"

—Herschel Fravel

339. IN HIS STEPS

"Christ also suffered for us, leaving us an example, that ye should follow his steps." *I Pet. 2:21*

Walking in Jesus' steps involves:

I. SABBATH OBSERVANCE AND CHURCH ATTENDANCE
("As his custom was, he went into the synagogue on the sabbath day." Luke 4:16.)

II. SOCIAL SERVICE
(Jesus "went about doing good." Acts 10:38.)

III. EVANGELISM
("Come ye after me, and I will make you to become fishers of men." Mark 1:17.)

IV. SELF-DENIAL, SACRIFICE
("If any man will come after me, let him deny himself, and take up his cross, and follow me." Matt. 16:24.)

340. THE CHRISTIAN IS RICH

". . . according as his divine power hath given unto us all things that pertain unto life and godliness." *II Pet. 1:3*

We are given:

1. A life—that is eternal (Rom. 6:23).

2. A relationship—which cannot be broken (Gal. 3:26).

3. A righteousness—which will not tarnish (II Cor. 5:21).

4. A peace—which the world can neither give nor take away (John 14:27).

5. An inheritance—which will never fade (I Pet. 1:4).

6. A home in heaven—prepared by the supreme Architect of the universe (John 14:3).

341. CHRIST IN PROPHECY

"The prophecy came not in old time by the will of man: but holy men of God spake as they were moved by the Holy Ghost."
II Pet. 1:21

I. The Place of His Birth (Mic. 5:2)
II. The Virgin Birth (Isa. 7:14)
III. A Name of the Christ (Isa. 7:14)
IV. The Sojourn in Egypt (Hos. 11:1)
V. The Forerunner (Isa. 40:3; Mal. 3:1)
VI. Miracles of Healing (Isa. 29:18; 53:4-5)
VII. The Triumphal Entry (Zech. 9:9)
VIII. The Thirty Pieces of Silver (Zech. 11:12-13)
IX. Numbered with Transgressors (Isa. 53:12)
X. The Resurrection (Ps. 16:10; Acts 2:27)

342. GROWTH IN GRACE

"Grow in grace, and in the knowledge of our Lord and Saviour Jesus Christ." *I Pet. 3:18*

Steps in this growth:
1. Grace (Jas. 4:6).
2. Sufficient grace (II Cor. 12:9).
3. Great grace (Acts 4:33).
4. More grace (Jas. 4:6).
5. Abundant grace (II Cor. 4:15).
6. Exceeding grace (II Cor. 9:14).
7. Exceeding riches of grace (Eph. 2:7).
8. Grace at its best (I Cor. 16:23).

343. THE WORD OF LIFE

"That which was from the beginning, which we have heard, which we have seen with our eyes, which we have looked upon, and our hands have handled, of the Word of life. . . ." *I John 1:1*

1. Revelation: "We have heard."
2. Observation: "We have seen."
3. Consideration: "We have looked."
4. Occupation: "Our hands have handled."

—W. B. C. Beggs, in *The Witness*

344. GOD IS LIGHT

"God is light, and in him is no darkness at all." *I John 1:5*

1. Light is purifying.
2. Light is vivifying.
3. Light is power.
4. Light is joyous.
5. Light is comforting.
6. Light is strengthening.
7. Light retards sin and crime.
8. God floods the tomb with light.
9. God is the Light of heaven.

345. LOVE IS OF GOD

"Beloved, let us love one another; for love is of God."
I John 4:7

Love
1. Is the evidence of life in Christ. (I John 3:14.)
2. Is the first "fruit of the Spirit." (Gal. 5:22.)
3. Is the fulfilling of the law. (Rom. 13:10.)
4. Is the "new commandment." (John 13:34.)
5. Is not to be in word only. (I John 3:18.)
6. Constrains to self-denying service. (II Cor. 5:14.)
7. Abides (I Cor. 13:13).

346. MANIFESTATIONS OF CHRISTIAN LIFE

"And this is the record, that God hath given to us eternal life, and this life is in his Son."
I John 5:11

Life
1. In the head—light (John 17:3).

2. In the heart—love (I John 3:14).
3. In the hands—labor (Eph. 6:6, 7).
4. In the feet—liberty (Gal. 5:1).
5. In the pocket—liberality (I John 3:17).
6. In the soul—glory (Col. 3:4).

—*Expositor*

347. FORMS OF IDOLATRY

"Little children, keep yourselves from idols." *I John 5:21*

The word "idol" as used here means anything that takes the place of God with us. Whatever a man puts his trust in, or gives his supreme affection to, is an idol, or a god.

I. Drunkenness, Gluttony, Lust, Are the Idols of Some.
   1. "Whose God is their belly." Phil. 3:19.
   2. This is idolatry in its lowest and most repulsive form.

II. Covetousness, Greed
   1. "Covetousness, which is idolatry" (Col. 3:5).
   2. The rich fool built larger barns.

III. Even Sacred Symbols May Become Idols.
   1. Some worship the cross instead of the Christ of the cross.
   2. Relics, medals, etc.

IV. What One Sees in a Mirror Can Be One's Idol.
   1. To spend more time on one's face than on one's spiritual life makes one something else—and less—than Christian.

348. HOW'S YOUR HEALTH?

"Beloved, I wish above all things that thou mayest prosper and be in health, even as thy soul prospereth." *III John 2.*

I. Some Symptoms of Spiritual Ill Health
   1. Low temperature; lack of warmth and vitality; no religious zeal or fervor
   2. High temperature; feverish living in an age of high pressure and high tension.
   3. Difficulty in breathing the atmosphere of prayer
   4. Failing appetite; no hunger for the Bread of life

II. Aids to Spiritual Health
   1. Proper feeding of the soul—we can't feed our souls on the husks of the world and thrive.
   2. Drink from "the Fountain of living waters."
   3. Mountain air: Transfiguration; Calvary.
   4. Exercise: "Exercise thyself . . . unto godliness."
   5. Rest: "They that wait upon the Lord shall renew their strength."

Application: Regularly see "the Great Physician."

349. IN THE SPIRIT

"I was in the Spirit on the Lord's day." *Rev. 1:10*

I. Live in the Spirit.
   (The Christian life—I John 4:9)

II. Walk in the Spirit.
   (The Christian walk—Gal. 5:25)

III. Pray in the Spirit.
   (Christian devotion—Eph. 6:18)

IV. Worship in the Spirit.
   (Christian priesthood—Phil. 3:3)

V. Love in the Spirit.
   (Christian brotherhood—Col. 1:8)

VI. Fruit of the Spirit.
   (Christian evidences—Eph. 5:9-10; Gal. 5:22-23)

350. VOICES OF JESUS

"His voice [was] as the sound of many waters." *Rev. 1:15*

1. Shepherd's voice: "Follow me."
2. Master's voice: "Occupy till I come."
3. Saviour's voice: "Come unto me."
4. Teacher's voice: "Learn of me."
5. Divine voice: "Hear ye him."
6. Friend's voice: "Ye are my friends."
7. Physician's voice: "Wilt thou be made whole?"

351. FAITHFULNESS REWARDED

"Be thou faithful unto death, and I will give thee a crown of life." *Rev. 2:10*

The religion of Christ:

1. Requires faithfulness
2. Requires personal faithfulness
3. Requires continual faithfulness
4. Richly rewards the faithful

352. SOMEONE'S AT THE DOOR

"Behold, I stand at the door, and knock; if any man hear my voice, and open the door, I will come in to him, and will sup with him, and he with me." *Rev. 3:20*

I. The Attitude of Jesus Before the Hearts of Men
   1. He stands. Patience.
   2. He knocks. Makes known his desire to enter.

II. Conditions upon Which He Will Enter
   1. "If any man hear my voice." Must listen.
   2. "And open the door." Must be opened by the individual. No lock or latch on Christ's side of the door.

III. What He Proposes to Do
   1. "I will come in." Any heart, any home, where welcome.
   2. "And will sup with him." Purposeful fellowship.

Application: When Christ is kept outside, there must be something wrong inside.

III
Special Days and Miscellaneous

353. THE UNTRODDEN PATH

(*New Year's*)

"Ye have not passed this way heretofore." *Josh. 3:4*

The Israelites were about to cross the river and enter the Promised Land.

I. THERE IS A PARALLEL BETWEEN THE POSITION OF THE ANCIENT ISRAELITES AND OURSELVES TODAY.
   1. The New Year is comparable to an unknown wilderness where none of us has ever been before.

II. THE NEW YEAR ADVENTURE CALLS FOR A GUIDE.
   1. The Lord's presence is promised.
   2. We are to follow "the ark of God."

III. WITH ABSOLUTE ASSURANCE THE CHRISTIAN CAN FACE INTO THE NEW YEAR AND SAY:
   1. "We know that all things work together for good to them that love God." Rom. 8:28.
   2. "Yea, though I walk through the valley of the shadow of death, I will fear no evil: for thou art with me; thy rod and thy staff they comfort me."

354. THE NEW YEAR'S JOURNEY —WHAT TO TAKE ALONG

"And now abideth faith, hope, charity, these three; but the greatest of these is charity." *I Cor. 13:13*

In the New Year you will need:

I. FAITH
   1. Faith in God; faith in him who said: "Lo, I am with you alway."
   2. Faith in the ultimate victory: "This is the victory that overcometh the world, even our faith."

II. HOPE
   1. Hope is the anchor that will enable us to ride out the storms of life.

III. LOVE
   1. Love is sunshine and will dispel gloom.
   2. Love is just another name for God. "God is love."
   3. We shall need God, and the love of God, each step of the way.

355. NEW YEAR'S RESOLUTIONS

"I press toward the mark." *Phil. 3:14*

I. I WOULD BE TRUE.
(For there are those who trust me.)

II. I WOULD BE PURE.
(For there are those who care.)

III. I WOULD BE STRONG.
(For there is much to suffer.)

IV. I WOULD BE BRAVE.
(For there is much to dare.)

V. I WOULD BE A LIVING CONSECRATION.
(Living for him whose holy name I bear.)

356. VALUES OF LENT

"Let us draw near with a true heart in full assurance of faith." *Heb. 10:22*

Lent is a time:

1. For beholding "the Lamb of God, which taketh away the sin of the world"

2. For "looking unto Jesus the author and finisher of our faith"

3. For self-examination: "Let a man examine himself."

4. To pray, "Create in me a clean heart, O God; and renew a right spirit within me."

5. For emphasis upon what we *take up*, not upon what we *give up*

6. For accepting the cross of Christ as well as the Christ of the cross

7. For *spiritual feasting*, not just *physical fasting*

8. To "draw near with a true heart in full assurance of faith"

357. THE KING WITH MANY CROWNS

(*Palm Sunday*)

"On his head were many crowns." *Rev. 19:12*

Palm Sunday is a paradox. Seemingly incompatible with meekness, humility, and simplicity of Jesus, and the spiritual nature of his kingdom.

Purpose: to dramatize a spiritual truth. Jesus was "King of kings." Disciples slow to understand. Sixty years pass, and John on Patmos has a vision of Christ with many crowns.

I. One Crown John Had Seen with His Own Eyes and Could Never Forget—the Crown of Thorns.
   1. The cruelty, bestiality, and fiendishness of it all were indelibly impressed upon his memory.
   2. Later, that crown became a thing to glory in—as Paul gloried in the cross.

II. A Second Crown Depicted Jesus' Lordship over Death.
   1. "O death, where is thy sting? O grave, where . . . ?"
   2. "He arose a victor o'er the dark domain."

III. A Third Crown Depicts Him in the Realm of Glory.
   1. John's vision of the great throng no man could number, white garments, palms, songs of victory, praise.
   2. Angels and archangels worshiping at his footstool.
   3. "Holy, holy, holy! all the saints adore Thee,
      Casting down their golden crowns around the glassy sea;
      Cherubim and seraphim falling down before Thee,
      Which wert, and art, and evermore shalt be."

IV. Another Crown—World Dominion.
   1. The kingdoms of this world are destined to become the kingdom of our Lord.
   2. "Jesus shall reign where'er the sun. . . ."
   3. The only solution to the ills of the world.

Application: The Palm Sunday pageant didn't end that day, but just began. We are in the processional. Some day we shall see the King in his beauty—the King with many crowns—the King of kings.

358. AT THE CROSS

(*Good Friday*)

"If we walk in the light, as he is in the light, we have fellowship one with another, and the blood of Jesus Christ his Son cleanseth us from all sin." *I John 1:7*

1. Here our ignorance of God is removed. Rom. 1:1-24.

2. Here a divine Substitute died in our stead. I Pet. 3:18.

3. Here the chains of our slavery are broken. Gal. 4:4-7.

4. Here a fountain for sin and uncleanness is opened. I John 1:5-9.

5. Here we get power from God for right living. Heb. 10:19-25.

6. Here we gain assurance of life after death. I Cor. 15.

359. THE RETURN OF SPRING

(*Easter*)

"For, lo, the winter is past, the rain is over and gone; the flowers appear on the earth; the time of the singing of birds is come."
Song of Songs 2:11-12

It is fitting that Easter should be celebrated in the spring, for spring is a resurrection. Note:

I. Spring Is a Hidden Force.
   1. In wintertime it is hard to

believe that nature can live again.
2. In the soul there is a hidden life that does not, cannot, perish.

II. SPRING REVEALS THE LIFE-GIVING POWER OF GOD.
1. No other way to explain springtime aside from the miraculous power of God.
2. The same is true of the resurrection of the soul.

III. SPRING IS A TYPE OF OUR RESURRECTION.
1. The same Lord who promises the return of the flowers and birds and summer blessings, also promises the resurrection and life of those who live and die in him.
2. "I am the resurrection and the life."

360. EASTER COMMANDS

"Come, see the place where the Lord lay. And go quickly, and tell his disciples that he is risen from the dead." *Matt. 28:6-7*

I. COME.
II. SEE.
III. GO.
IV. TELL.

361. MOTHERHOOD AT ITS BEST

(*Mother's Day*)

"Her children arise up, and call her blessed; her husband also, and he praiseth her." *Prov. 31:28*

The "good-mother" chapter of the Bible is without doubt the thirty-first chapter of Proverbs, where Lemuel pays tribute to his own mother. An analysis of good motherhood as contained in this chapter reveals the following qualities:

1. Virtue (verse 10)
2. Industry (verse 13)
3. Economy (verse 16)
4. Benevolence (verse 20)
5. Ability to be a good helpmeet (verse 26)
6. Intelligence (verse 26)
7. Love of home (verse 27)
8. Reverence and religion (verse 30)

362. DEVOUT MOTHERS

"His mother kept all these sayings in her heart." *Luke 2:51*

Some great mothers:
1. Sarah (Gen. 21:6)
2. Hannah (I Sam. 1:22)
3. Elizabeth (Luke 1:41)
4. Mary (Luke 1:46)
5. Eunice (II Tim. 1:5)

363. CHRISTIAN HOME LIFE

"I call to remembrance the unfeigned faith that is in thee, which dwelt first in thy grandmother Lois, and thy mother Eunice; and I am persuaded that in thee also." *II Tim. 1:5*

A generation ago many homes had hanging upon the wall a motto with these words: "Christ is the Head of this house; the unseen Host at every meal; the silent Listener to every conversation."

Here is a formula for happy Christian home life:

I. "CHRIST IS THE HEAD OF THIS HOUSE."
1. That would settle the question, "Who's boss?"
2. Every domestic problem can be solved if taken to Christ, the head of the house.

II. "THE UNSEEN HOST AT EVERY MEAL."
1. Though unseen, his presence is real, and should be felt.
2. "Host." He provides food for our bodies as well as our souls.

III. "THE SILENT LISTENER TO EVERY CONVERSATION"
1. What a difference it makes in a home when it is realized that Christ hears all that is said!

2. No angry words, no unkind gossip, no vulgarity

Application: When Christ said, "I stand at the door, and knock," he meant the door of the home as well as the heart.

364. PETER'S SERMON ON THE DAY OF PENTECOST

"Peter, standing up with the eleven, lifted up his voice, and said unto them, Ye men of Judaea, and all ye that dwell at Jerusalem, be this known unto you, and hearken to my words." *Acts 2:14*

Read Acts 2:14-41.

1. It magnified the Scriptures. (Verses 14-21.)
2. It emphasized the gospel. (Verses 22-32.)
3. It glorified the Lord. (Verses 33-36.)
4. It produced conviction. (Verse 37.)
5. It showed the way. (Verse 38.)
6. It promised much. (Verses 39-40.)
7. It brought results. (Verse 41.)

—James Ostema

365. WORLD-WIDE COMMUNION

"We are all partakers of that one bread." *I Cor. 10:17*

The fellowship of the Holy Communion service is threefold:

I. IT IS A FELLOWSHIP WITH CHRIST HIMSELF.
   1. "Where two or three are gathered together in my name, there am I in the midst of them." Matt. 18:20.
   2. The Emmaus story

II. IT IS A FELLOWSHIP OF KINDRED SPIRITS.
   1. "Behold, how good and how pleasant it is for brethren to dwell together in unity!" Ps. 133:1.
   2. "Blest be the tie that binds."

III. IT IS A FELLOWSHIP WITH THE CHURCH UNIVERSAL AND SPIRITUAL.
   1. World Communion
   2. All colors, in all climes
   3. The holy catholic Church—meaning of the term

366. THANKS-LIVING

"If ye love me, keep my commandments." *John 14:15*

There are two principal ways of showing we have grateful hearts:

I. THANKS-GIVING
   1. Testimony
   2. Song
   3. Public worship

II. THANKS-LIVING
   1. "Walk worthy. . . ."
   2. Text
   3. "Why call ye me, Lord, Lord, and do not the things which I say?"
   4. "Prove the sincerity of your love."

367. UNWISE MEN

(*Advent*)

"See then that ye walk circumspectly, not as fools, but as wise, redeeming the time, because the days are evil." *Eph. 5:15-16*

A man is unwise:

I. WHEN HE FAILS TO FOLLOW THE LEADERSHIP OF GOD'S SPIRIT
   1. It was not so much a star that led the Magi to Christ as the Spirit of God.
   2. After their worship, they departed another way, "being warned of God in a dream."

II. WHEN HE NEGLECTS THE WORSHIP OF CHRIST
   1. The Magi were busy men, and could easily have used this fact as an excuse for remaining at home.
   2. Wise men put first things first.
   3. A man is unwise when he lightly esteems the holy

privilege of worshiping Christ.

III. WHEN HE FAILS TO GIVE GIFTS TO CHRIST

IV. WHEN HE SEES NO POTENTIALITIES IN A LITTLE CHILD

368. WHY READ THE BIBLE?

(*Universal Bible Sunday*)

"[They] searched the scriptures daily, whether those things were so." *Acts 17:11*

I. SOME READ THE BIBLE FOR ARGUMENT'S SAKE.
  1. Destructive critics

II. SOME READ THE BIBLE JUST TO BE ABLE TO SAY THEY HAVE READ IT.
  1. The important thing is not that you went through the Bible. Did it go through you?

III. SOME READ THE BIBLE TO GET SOMETHING INTO IT.
  1. Read with prejudice, to prove a theory, etc.

IV. SOME READ IT TO GET SOMETHING OUT OF IT.
  1. It is an inexhaustible mine of treasure.

V. THE BEST MOTIVE FOR BIBLE READING IS TO GET TO SOMEONE—CHRIST.
  1. "They are they which testify of me."
  2. The Bible is history—His story.

Application: The text.

369. CHRISTMAS GIVING

(*Christmas*)

"When they had opened their treasures, they presented unto him gifts." *Matt. 2:11*

The giving of gifts at Christmas has a good biblical background. "God so loved the world that he gave. . . ." The Magi gave gifts. Text.

I. CHRISTMAS IS A TIME FOR GIVING UP.
  1. It is a time for self-surrender to Christ. "They first gave their own selves."

II. CHRISTMAS IS A TIME FOR GIVING IN.
  1. Sincere surrender to Christ puts us into his church, his fellowship, his kingdom.

III. CHRISTMAS IS A TIME FOR GIVING OUT.
  1. Out of loving hearts we give to the poor.
  2. The best evidence of the Christmas spirit in the heart lies not in decorations, music, pageantry, gift swapping, tinsel, lights, but in sharing with the unfortunate in Christ's name.
  3. General Booth's telegram: "Others."

370. CHRIST CROWDED OUT

"There was no room for them in the inn." *Luke 2:7*

What was true in Bethlehem on that first Christmas in the long ago is all too true in our modern world.

There is little room for Christ in:

1. Business
2. Pleasures
3. Conversations
4. Politics
5. World Councils
6. Modern homes
7. Some churches
8. Many hearts

371. THE SHEPHERDS AND THE ANGELS

"And there were in the same country shepherds abiding in the field, keeping watch over their flock by night." *Luke 2:8*

Read Luke 2:8-14.

I. THE CIRCUMSTANCES OF THE ANNOUNCEMENT
  1. The persons to whom the announcement was made—shepherds about their daily work

2. The time—by night
3. The heralds—the angel of the Lord and a multitude of the heavenly host

II. The Angel's Proclamation
1. The Saviour
2. Born
3. To you
4. That he might reveal God
5. That he might be our example
6. That he might die for us

III. The Angel Chorus
1. Glory to God in the highest.
2. On earth peace.

—Alexander Maclaren

372. CHRISTMAS AFTERMATH

"The shepherds returned, glorifying and praising God for all the things that they had heard and seen, as it was told unto them."
Luke 2:20

I. The Worship of Christ Enables Us to Sing at Our Toil.

II. The Worship of Christ Makes Better Workmen of Us.

III. The Love of Christ Enables Us to Sing Songs at Midnight.
1. The shepherds
2. Paul and Silas in prison

IV. The Real Values of Christmas Become Apparent after Christmas.

373. DUTIES OF CITIZENSHIP

"Render . . . unto Caesar the things which be Caesar's."
Luke 20:25

I. Know Your Rulers. (I Thess. 5:12.)

II. "Remember Them Which Have the Rule over You." (Heb. 13:7.)

III. Pray for Rulers. (I Tim. 2:2.)

IV. Yield to Authority. (Heb. 13:17.)

V. Salute [Respect] Rulers. (Heb. 13:24.)

VI. Pay Just Taxes. (Luke 20:25.)

374. THE CHURCH AND PATRIOTISM

"He loveth our nation, and he hath built us a synagogue."
Luke 7:5

Wise patriotism concerns itself with the religious welfare of the nation.

I. The Nation Is Indebted to the Sanctuary for the Best Elements in Its Life.

II. The Nation Is Indebted to the Sanctuary for the Indispensable Conditions of Its Progress.
(Reforms; ideals; character supplied by the church.)

III. The Nation Is Indebted to the Sanctuary for the Supply of Its Best Citizens.

—B. J. Gibbon

375. MISSIONS

"Go ye therefore. . . ."
Matt. 28:19

Elements involved in missions:
1. The missionary message (Rom. 1:14-16)
2. The missionary passion (Rom. 9:1-3)
3. The missionary argument (Rom. 10:11-15)
4. The missionary ambition (Rom. 15:18-21)

376. THE LORD'S PRAYER REVISED

(*For use by those who do not believe in missions*)

Underscored words must be eliminated.

Our Father which art in heaven,
Hallowed be thy name.
Thy kingdom come.
Thy will be done in earth,

As it is in heaven.
Give us [me] this day our [my] daily bread.
And forgive us [me] our [my] debts,
As we forgive our debtors.
And lead us [me] not into temptation,
But deliver us [me] from evil:
For thine is the kingdom,
And the power,
And the glory,
For ever. Amen.

377. THE IMPORTANCE OF THE SACRAMENT

"He that loveth me not keepeth not my sayings." *John 14:24*

Wilful failure to commune suggests:

I. BASE INGRATITUDE
   1. About to die for us, Jesus asked that we do this in remembrance of him.
   2. A simple request

II. CONTEMPT FOR CHRIST
   1. It suggests we do not take him seriously.
   2. Comparable to contempt of court—failure to appear in answer to a summons.

III. A FORM OF TREASON
   1. As patriots are expected to show respect for the national flag, so the Christian in the sacrament salutes "the bloodstained banner of the cross."
   2. "Stand up and be counted."

IV. BREAKING AN ENGAGEMENT WITH CHRIST
   1. "Where two or three are gathered together in my name, there am I in the midst of them."
   2. What Thomas missed by his absence from the Upper Room!

V. SOMETHING VITAL FADING FROM OUR LIVES
   1. To treat lightly this sacred feast indicates backsliding.
   2. The fading out of spiritual values

Application: If it was important for Paul to walk many miles to participate in the sacrament, it is likewise important for us.

378. THE LORD'S SUPPER

"This do in remembrance of me."
I Cor. 11:24

I. ITS AUTHOR—"THE LORD JESUS"

II. WHEN INSTITUTED—"THE SAME NIGHT IN WHICH HE WAS BETRAYED"

III. THE ELEMENTS USED
   1. Broken bread: "This is my body, which is broken for you."
   2. The wine: "This cup is the new testament in my blood."

IV. THE PURPOSE
   1. "In remembrance of me"
   2. Many forget.

V. A WORD OF CAUTION
   1. "Let a man examine himself." (Verses 28, 29.)
   2. Examine self, not others.

379. THE LORD'S SUPPER

"This do ye, as oft as ye drink it, in remembrance of me. For as often as ye eat this bread, and drink this cup, ye do shew the Lord's death till he come."
I Cor. 11:25-26

I. DIVINELY COMMANDED
("This do ye." Verse 25.)

II. A COMMEMORATIVE EVENT
("In remembrance of me"—verse 25)

III. A PROCLAMATION OF A GLORIOUS FACT
("Ye do shew the Lord's death." Verse 26.)

IV. A CONTINUING OBLIGATION
("Till he come"—verse 26)

380. RALLY DAY OUTFIT

"Put on the whole armour of God." *Eph. 6:11*

I. Shod to Walk
(Deut. 33:25; Eph. 6:15)
II. Girded to Serve
(Ps. 18:32; John 13:4)
III. Armed to Fight
(Eph. 6:10; I Tim. 6:12)

—G. B. F. Hallock

381. LOCATING GOD

"Oh that I knew where I might find him!" *Job 23:3*

God is:

1. Before us (Isa. 48:17; Ps. 139:5; Isa. 52:12)
2. Behind us (Isa. 30:21; Ps. 139:5; Isa. 52:12)
3. To the right (Ps. 16:8; 18:35; Job 23:9)
4. To the left (Job 23:9)
5. Above (Ps. 36:7)
6. Beneath (Deut. 33:27)
7. Within (I Cor. 3:16)
8. Around (Ps. 125:2)

—J. H. Sammis

382. SAINTS WHERE THEY SHOULD NOT BE

"Blessed is the man that walketh not in the counsel of the ungodly, nor standeth in the way of sinners, nor sitteth in the seat of the scornful." *Ps. 1:1*

1. A backsliding believer—Abram in Egypt (Gen. 12:10)
2. A silenced witness—Lot in Sodom (Gen. 14:12)
3. A lustful king—David on the house roof (II Sam. 11:2)
4. A discouraged prophet—Elijah under the juniper tree (I Kings 19:4)
5. A disobedient servant—Jonah headed for Tarshish (Jon. 1:2)
6. A preacher in Doubting Castle—John the Baptist (Matt. 11:2-3)
7. A conscience-stricken disciple—Peter warming by the enemy's fire (Luke 22:55)

383. THE FACE OF JESUS

"When thou saidst, Seek ye my face; my heart said unto thee, Thy face, Lord, will I seek." *Ps. 27:8*

The Bible is an album in which we catch many glimpses of the face of Jesus.

1. A strong face (Luke 9:51)
2. A face bowed in prayer (Matt. 26:39)
3. An insulted face (Matt. 26:67; Mark 14:65)
4. An injured face (Luke 22:64)
5. A shining face (Matt. 17:2)
6. A glorious face (II Cor. 4:6)
7. An awe-inspiring face (Rev. 6:16; 20:11)
8. Face to face with him in heaven (Rev. 22:4)

384. CHARACTERISTICS OF THE WICKED

"The transgression of the wicked saith within my heart, that there is no fear of God before his eyes." *Ps. 36:1*

Read Psalm 36.

A wicked person

1. Lacks reverence for God (verse 1).
2. Indulges in self-flattery (verse 2).
3. Is given to evil and deceitful talk (verse 3).
4. Is unwise (verse 3).
5. Leaves good undone (verse 3).
6. Studies up mischief (verse 4).
7. Chooses the wrong road (verse 4).
8. Sees no horror of sin (verse 4).
9. Comes to a sad end (verse 12).

385. THE WHEREABOUTS OF GOD

"Where is thy God?" *Ps. 42:3*

Our God is:

1. Before us (Deut. 1:30)
2. Behind us (Isa. 52:12)
3. Above us (Ps. 18:16)
4. Beneath us (Deut. 33:27)
5. Around us (Ps. 125:2)

386. THE BULWARKS OF ZION

"Walk about Zion, and go around about her: tell the towers thereof. Mark ye well her bulwarks, consider her palaces; that ye may tell it to the generation following."
Ps. 48:12-13

In these days of toppling thrones, disintegrating empires, abolition of moral standards, and flaunting of wise and wholesome traditions, some are pessimistic as to the future of the Church.

I. THERE WILL ALWAYS BE THE CHURCH.
   1. "The gates of hell shall not prevail against it." (Matt. 16:18.)
   2. "Crowns and thrones may perish,
      Kingdoms rise and wane,
      But the Church of Jesus
      Constant will remain."

II. THE BULWARKS OF THE CHURCH
   1. God: "A mighty fortress is our God." (Luther.) "God is our refuge and strength." (Ps. 46:1.)
   2. Jesus Christ: "Chief corner stone" (Eph. 2:20); "same yesterday, . . . to day, . . . for ever" (Heb. 13:8).
   3. The Word of God: "The grass withereth, the flower fadeth: but the word of our God shall stand for ever" (Isa. 40:8).
   4. Love: "But now abideth faith, hope, love" (I Cor. 13:13, A.S.V.).
   5. Truth: "Truth is mighty and it will prevail" (Esdras, Apocrypha). "Truth, crushed to earth, shall rise again" (Bryant).

387. PRAISE

"Whoso offereth praise glorifieth me: and to him that ordereth his conversation aright will I shew the salvation of God."
Ps. 50:23

Praise is:

1. The first song of creation (Job 38:7)
2. The first song of redemption (Luke 2:13-14, 20)
3. The first testimony of the saved (Acts 3:8-9)
4. A powerful testimony to the unsaved (Acts 16:25)
5. The employment of heaven (Rev. 19:5)
6. To be continuous (Heb. 13:15)

—C. E. Paxton

388. MAN'S SINFUL NATURE

"Behold, I was shapen in iniquity; and in sin did my mother conceive me."
Ps. 51:5

By nature we are:

1. Evil in our thoughts continually (Gen. 6:5)
2. Unclean (Job 14:4)
3. "As filthy rags" (Isa. 64:6)
4. "Deceitful . . . and desperately wicked" (Jer. 17:9)
5. All under sin (Rom. 3:9-23)
6. "The children of wrath" (Eph. 2:3)
7. "Aliens from the commonwealth of Israel" (Eph. 2:12)
8. "Alienated from the life of God" (Eph. 4:18)
9. Dead in trespasses and sins (Col. 2:13)

389. GOOD OUT OF EVIL

"Surely the wrath of man shall praise thee."
Ps. 76:10

Through the centuries God has been overruling the wrath of man to His praise:

I. JOSEPH MALTREATED BY HIS BRETHREN
   (Joseph's valedictory: "Ye thought evil against me; but God meant it unto good . . . to save much people alive.")

II. PHARAOH'S EDICT THAT JEWISH BABIES BE SLAIN
   (Moses reared and educated in Pharaoh's court for leadership of the Israelites.)

III. Goliath's Challenge Seemingly Calamitous
(God-fearing David slays the giant and wins respect for the God of Israel.)

IV. Daniel Cast into the Lions' Den
(Daniel: "My God hath sent his angel, and hath shut the lions' mouths.")

V. Jesus Condemned to Death on the Cross
(Millions glory in "The Old Rugged Cross," the central symbol of the Christian faith.)

VI. Persecution in the Early Church
(The disciples "went every where preaching the word.")

VII. Paul Chained to Roman Guards
(The guards, converted, became evangelists and missionaries.)

VIII. John Tetzel's Sale of Indulgences
(Martin Luther goes into action—the result, Protestantism.)

390. THE VOYAGE OF LIFE

"So he bringeth them unto their desired haven." *Ps. 107:30*

For the voyage we need:

1. A captain who is wise—Jesus (Heb. 2:10)

2. A chart that is safe—the Bible (Ps. 119:9, 105)

3. A compass which is true—the Holy Spirit (John 16:13)

4. A cable that is strong—faith (Heb. 11:1)

5. An anchor that reassures—hope (Heb. 6:19)

6. A crew who are capable—preachers and teachers (II Tim. 2:15)

7. Voyagers who are happy—Christians (Heb. 11:13-14; Col. 3:16)

—*500 Bible Studies*

391. WISDOM

"Happy is the man that findeth wisdom, and the man that getteth understanding." *Prov. 3:13*

I. Wisdom Defined
1. Job 28:28
2. Prov. 9:10

II. Worth of Wisdom
1. Job 28:13-19
2. Prov. 8:11

III. Source of Wisdom
1. Job 28:20-23

IV. Our Duty to Seek Wisdom
1. Prov. 8:33-35

V. Christ, the Embodiment of Wisdom
1. Eph. 3:8-11

VI. Prayers for Wisdom
1. Solomon: I Kings 3:9
2. Paul: Eph. 1:15-23; Col. 1:9-11

VII. How to Secure Wisdom
1. Prayer—Jas. 1:5
2. Bible—II Tim. 3:13-17
3. Holy Spirit—John 14:26

—H. M. Morey

392. PRAYER CAN BE A WASTE OF TIME

"The Lord is far from the wicked: but he heareth the prayer of the righteous." *Prov. 15:29*

It is made clear in Scripture that some people waste time when they pray.

Some instances:

I. Sinners
1. Text
2. Isa. 59:2: "Your sins have hid his face from you, that he will not hear."
3. John 9:31: "God heareth not sinners."

II. The Unteachable
1. Prov. 28:9: "He that turneth his ear from hearing the law, even his prayer shall be abomination."

III. The Uncharitable
1. Prov. 21:13: "Whoso stoppeth his ears at the cry of

the poor, he also shall cry himself, but shall not be heard."
2. "Why call ye me, Lord, Lord, and do not the things which I say?"

IV. THE SELF-RIGHTEOUS
1. Luke 18:9-12: the Pharisee
2. Luke 10:30-37: priest and Levite

393. THE TONGUE

"Death and life are in the power of the tongue." *Prov. 18:21*

The tongue is like:
1. A steed (Jas. 3:3)
2. A sword (Ps. 57:4)
3. A serpent (Ps. 140:3)
4. Fire (Jas. 3:6)

—James Stalker

394. THE EVILS OF STRONG DRINK

"Wine is a mocker, strong drink is raging: and whosoever is deceived thereby is not wise." *Prov. 20:1*

Strong drink leads to:

I. SHAME
1. Example of Noah (Gen. 9:21)
2. Example of Lot (Gen. 19:33)

II. FOLLY
1. Example of Ahasuerus (Esth. 1:10-11)

III. DEFEAT
1. Example of Benhadad (I Kings 20:16-20)

IV. POVERTY
1. Warnings of Solomon (Prov. 23:21)

V. TROUBLE
1. Warnings of Solomon (Prov. 23:29-30)

VI. SACRILEGE
1. Example of Belshazzar (Dan. 5:1-5)

VII. ETERNAL REJECTION OF GOD
1. I Cor. 6:10

—*Curiosities of the Bible*

395. WHAT THE WELL-DRESSED CHRISTIAN WILL WEAR

"Awake, awake; put on thy strength, O Zion; put on thy beautiful garments, O Jerusalem." *Isa. 52:1*

I. THE SOUL'S GARMENTS SHOULD BE WHITE.
1. Eccles. 9:8
2. Isa. 1:18
3. Rev. 3:5

II. "BE CLOTHED WITH HUMILITY."
1. I Pet. 5:5
2. Matt. 5:5

III. "THE MANTLE OF CHARITY"
1. Col. 3:14
2. I Pet. 4:8

IV. "THE GARMENT OF PRAISE"
1. Isa. 61:3
2. Ps. 33:1

396. ABUNDANT PARDON

"Let the wicked forsake his way, and the unrighteous man his thoughts: and let him return unto the Lord, and he will have mercy upon him; and to our God, for he will abundantly pardon." *Isa. 55:7*

I. A CALL TO REPENTANCE
("Forsake his way." See Prov. 14:12.)

II. AN INVITATION TO GRACE
("Return unto the Lord." See Luke 15:18.)

III. A PROMISE OF MERCY
("He will have mercy." See Eph. 2:4.)

IV. A GRACIOUS PARDON
("He will abundantly pardon." See Neh. 9:17.)

397. WHEN REPENTANCE IS GENUINE

"Bring forth therefore fruits meet for repentance." *Matt. 3:8*

Characteristics of sincere repentance:

1. Humility (II Chron. 7:14; Jas. 4:9-10).

2. Self-abhorrence (Job 42:6).
3. Confession (Lev. 26:40; Job 33:27).
4. Faith (Matt. 21:32; Mark 1:15; Acts 20:21).
5. Prayer (I Kings 8:33; Acts 8:22).
6. Conversion (Acts 3:19; 26:20).
7. Turning from sin (II Chron. 6:26).
8. Turning from idols (Ezek. 14:6; I Thess. 1:9).
9. Greater zeal in the pathway of duty (II Cor. 7:11).
10. "Fruits meet for repentance" (Matt. 3:8).

398. THE BLESSED MEEK

"Blessed are the meek: for they shall. . . ." *Matt. 5:5*

The meek
1. Shall be satisfied (Ps. 22:26).
2. Shall be guided (Ps. 25:9).
3. Shall be taught (Ps. 25:9).
4. Shall inherit the earth (Ps. 37:11; Matt. 5:5).
5. Shall be saved (Ps. 76:9).
6. Shall be lifted up (Ps. 147:6).
7. Shall be beautiful with salvation (Ps. 149:4).

—J. M. H.

399. LAID UP

"Lay up for yourselves treasures in heaven." *Matt. 6:20*

1. "Lay up" the words of God in the heart. (Job 22:22.)
2. God's goodness "laid up" for them that fear him (Ps. 31:19).
3. Hope "laid up" in heaven (Col. 1:5).
4. A crown of righteousness "laid up" (II Tim. 4:8).

400. COME TO JESUS! FOR WHAT?

"Come unto me." *Matt. 11:28*

Come unto Jesus for:
1. Pardon (Eph. 1:5-7)
2. Comfort (John 14:16-18)
3. Health (Matt. 8:16-17)
4. Strength (Phil. 4:13)
5. Holiness (John 15:4-5)
6. Peace (John 14:27)
7. Joy (John 15:10-11)
8. Rest (Matt. 11:28)
9. Happiness (Prov. 13:17-18)
10. Eternal life (John 6:47)

—*Curiosities of the Bible*

401. PROGRESSIVE JOY

"Enter thou into the joy of thy Lord." *Matt. 25:21*

1. Joy (Gal. 5:22).
2. Great joy (Luke 2:10).
3. Exceeding joy (I Pet. 4:13).
4. Exceeding great joy (Matt. 2:10).
5. Abundance of joy (II Cor. 8:2).
6. Fullness of joy (John 15:11).
7. Unspeakable joy (I Pet. 1:8).
8. Everlasting joy (Isa. 35:10).

—T. B.

402. THE SOWER

"Behold, there went out a sower to sow." *Mark 4:3*

I. What to Sow
  1. Precious seed (Ps. 126:6).
  2. The Word (Mark 4:14).
II. How to Sow
  1. In tears (Ps. 126:5-6).
  2. Intelligently (Jer. 4:3)
III. Where to Sow
  1. "Beside *all* waters" (Isa. 32:20).
  2. "All the world" (Mark 16:15)
IV. When to Sow
  1. In the morning (Eccl. 11:6).
  2. In the evening (Eccl. 11:6).
V. Joy of Harvest
  1. Ps. 126:5-6
  2. Gal. 6:9
  3. John 4:36

403. DAY BY DAY

"Give us day by day our daily bread." *Luke 11:3*

1. Daily renewing of the inner man (II Cor. 4:16).
2. Daily reading of the Word (Neh. 8:18; Acts 17:11).
3. Daily prayer to the Lord (Ps. 86:3).
4. Daily praising of the Lord (Ps. 72:15).
5. Daily exhortation of one another (Heb. 3:13).
6. Daily cross bearing (Luke 9:23).
7. Daily effort at soul winning (Acts 2:47).

404. WHY NOT COME TO CHRIST?

"Come; for all things are now ready." *Luke 14:17*

1. We are *permitted* to come. (Rev. 22:17; Isa. 55:1).
2. We are *invited* to come. (Matt. 11:28.)
3. We are *entreated* to come. (II Cor. 5:20.)
4. We are *commanded* to come. (I John 3:23; Heb. 11:6.)
5. We are *compelled* to come. (Luke 14:23.)
6. We are *promised* salvation if we come. (John 3:16; John 6:37.)
7. We are *warned* of the consequences of not coming. (Mark 16:16; Heb. 2:3.)

405. THE CHRISTIAN'S COMMITMENT

"Whosoever . . . forsaketh not all that he hath, he cannot be my disciple." *Luke 14:33*

Statements of commitment:

1. "I take God the Father to be my God." (See I Thess. 1:9.)
2. "I take God the Son to be my Saviour." (See Acts 5:31.)
3. "I take God the Holy Ghost to be my Sanctifier." (See I Pet. 1:2.)
4. "I take the Word of God to be my rule." (See II Tim. 3:16-17.)
5. "I take the people of God to be my people." (See Ruth 1:16-17.)
6. "I likewise dedicate my whole self to the Lord." (See Rom. 14:7-8.)
7. "And I do this deliberately (Josh. 24:15); sincerely (II Cor. 1:12); freely (Ps. 110:3); and forever (Rom. 8:35-39)."

—*Curiosities of the Bible*

406. WHAT BECOMES OF THE BELIEVER'S SINS?

". . . and that repentance and remission of sins should be preached in his name among all nations, beginning at Jerusalem." *Luke 24:47*

The believer's sins are:

1. Borne by Christ (I Pet. 2:24).
2. Nailed to the cross (Col. 2:13-14).
3. Removed from us (Ps. 103:12).
4. Blotted out (Isa. 44:22).
5. Cast into the depths of the sea (Mic. 7:19).
6. Cast behind God's back (Isa. 38:17).
7. Forgiven (Ps. 78:38).
8. Forgotten (Isa. 43:25).

—Arthur J. Smith

407. THIS IS THE LIFE

"In him was life; and the life was the light of men." *John 1:4*

The ideal life is:

1. A life of holiness (I Thess. 5:22; II Tim. 2:19).
2. A life of prayer (I Tim. 2:8; I Thess. 5:17).
3. A life of faith (Heb. 11:6; Col. 1:23).
4. A life of self-denial (Matt. 5:29; Gal. 5:24).
5. A life of separation from the world (Exod. 32:26).
6. A life of consecration (I Chron. 29:5*b*; Rom. 12:1).
7. A life of service (Deut. 10:12; Luke 16:13).

—*500 Bible Studies*

408. EUREKA!

"We have found him."
John 1:45

What they find who find Christ:
1. Life (John 11:25).
2. Liberty (John 8:36).
3. Treasure (Matt. 13:44).
4. Rest (Matt. 11:28-29).
5. Refuge (Isa. 32:2).
6. Joy (John 17:13).

409. THE GOOD SHEPHERD

"I am the good shepherd: the good shepherd giveth his life for the sheep." *John 10:11*

The Good Shepherd
1. Knows his sheep (John 10:14, 27).
2. Calls (John 10:3).
3. Gathers (Isa. 40:11; John 10:16).
4. Guides (Ps. 23:3; John 10:3-4).
5. Feeds (Ps. 23:1-2; John 10:9).
6. Cherishes tenderly (Isa. 40:11).
7. Protects, preserves (Jer. 31:10; John 10:28).
8. Lays down life for (Zech. 13:7; Acts 20:28).
9. Gives eternal life to (John 10:28).

—R. A. Torrey

410. THE WAY

"Jesus saith unto him, I am the way." *John 14:6*

Christ is:
1. The Way of salvation (Acts 16:17).
2. The Way of life (Jer. 21:8).
3. The Way of peace (Luke 1:79).

411. CHRIST OUR LIFE

"Jesus saith unto him, I am . . . the life." *John 14:6*

Christ is:
1. The Bread of life (John 6:35).
2. The Fountain of life (Ps. 36:9).
3. The Tree of life (Rev. 2:7).
4. The Light of life (John 8:12).
5. The Path of life (Ps. 16:11).
6. The Word of life (I John 1:1).
7. The Prince of life (Acts 3:15).

412. THE DIVINE GUIDE

"He will guide you into all truth." *John 16:13*

I. We Need a Guide.
(I Chron. 29:15).
II. He Knows the Road.
(Job 23:10.)
III. He Can Bring Us to Glory.
(Heb. 2:10.)
IV. He Accompanies Us All the the Way.
(Ps. 23:4; Matt. 28:20.)
V. He Reassures the Traveler
(Ps. 37:23.)
VI. He Brings Us Home at Last.
(Ps. 107:30.)

413. ALL IN THE FAMILY

". . . that they all may be one; as thou, Father, art in me, and I in thee, that they also may be one in us." *John 17:21*

I. God Is Our Father (Matt. 6:9.)
II. Children in the Same Family (John 11:52; Ps. 133:1).
III. Pupils in the Same School (Acts 20:7).
IV. In the Same Flock (John 10:16).
V. The Same Church Home (Prov. 22:2).
VI. The Family Name (Eph. 3:14-15; Acts 11:26).
VII. Same Home Over There (John 14:2-3).

414. CHARACTERISTICS OF GOD

"My Lord and my God."
John 20:28

He is the God of:

1. Truth (Deut. 32:4).
2. All grace (I Pet. 5:10).
3. Peace (Phil. 4:9).
4. Love (II Cor. 13:11).
5. All comfort (II Cor. 1:3).
6. Patience (Rom. 15:5).
7. Hope (Rom. 15:13).
8. Glory (Acts 7:2).
9. Judgment (Isa. 30:18).
10. Mercies (II Cor. 1:3).

—*Notes for Bible Readings*

415. WHAT BECOMES OF A PENITENT'S SINS?

"Repent, and be baptized every one of you in the name of Jesus Christ for the remission of sins."
Acts 2:38

A penitent's sins are:

1. Laid upon Jesus (Isa. 53:6; Heb. 9:28).
2. Forgiven (Eph. 1:7).
3. Removed from us as far as the east is from the west (Ps. 103:12).
4. Washed away (Acts 22:16).
5. Remembered no more (Heb. 10:17).

416. WHAT IS A CHRISTIAN?

"The disciples were called Christians." *Acts 11:26*

A Christian is:

1. A sinner—saved by grace (I Tim. 1:15; Eph. 2:8).
2. A son—born into the family of God (John 1:12; I John 3:2).
3. A saint—called to holiness (Rom. 1:6; Eph. 5:3).
4. A servant—working for Christ (John 12:26; Col. 3:24).

417. NO EXCUSE

"They are without excuse."
Rom. 1:20

I. THE EXCUSE OF UNBELIEF
(John 3:12)

II. THE EXCUSE OF FEAR
(Luke 19:11-27)

III. THE EXCUSE OF PROCRASTINATION
(Acts 24:22-27)

IV. THE EXCUSE OF FALSE MODESTY
(Num. 13:26-33)

V. THE EXCUSE OF OTHER BUSINESS
(Luke 14:16-24)

VI. THEREFORE MAKE NO EXCUSES
(John 4:31-38)

VII. WILL OUR EXCUSES STAND?

418. MAN A SINNER

"Wherefore, as by one man sin entered into the world, and death by sin; and so death passed upon all men, for that all have sinned."
Rom. 5:12

I. NONE RIGHTEOUS
(Rom. 3:10).

II. ALL HAVE SINNED AND COME SHORT
(Rom. 3:23).

III. ALL UNDER SIN
(Gal. 3:22).

IV. CHILDREN OF WRATH
(Eph. 2:1-3).

V. UNCLEAN
(Job 14:4; Isa. 64:6).

VI. SHAPEN IN INIQUITY
(Ps. 51:5).

VII. EVIL CONTINUALLY
(Gen. 6:5).

VIII. DESPERATELY WICKED
(Jer. 17:9).

—*Notes for Bible Readings*

419. THE TRANSFORMATIONS OF GRACE

"Be ye transformed."
Rom. 12:2

WHAT WE WERE

Children of wrath (Eph. 2:3)
Children of disobedience (Col. 3:6)
Dead in sin (Eph. 2:5)
In darkness (Acts 26:18)
Without Christ (Eph. 2:12)
In bondage (Ezra 9:9)
Aliens and strangers (Eph. 2:12)

WHAT WE ARE

Children of God (Rom. 8:16)
Obedient children (I Pet. 1:14)

Alive unto God (Rom. 6:11)
Made nigh (Eph. 2:13)
Christ in you (Col. 1:27)
Called to liberty (Gal. 5:1)
A royal priesthood (I Pet. 2:9)
—*Outlines of Scripture Studies*

420. CHRIST OUR ROCK

"And that Rock was Christ."
I Cor. 10:4

Christ is:

1. The Rock of salvation (II Sam. 22:47).
2. The Rock of shelter (Isa. 32:2).
3. The Rock of stability (Ps. 40:2).
4. The Rock of song (Isa. 42:11).

421. YIELD NOT TO TEMPTATION

"God is faithful, who will not suffer you to be tempted above that ye are able." *I Cor. 10:13*

Christians should:

1. Resist temptation in faith. (Eph. 6:16; I Pet. 5:9).
2. Watch against temptation (Matt. 26:41; I Pet. 5:8).
3. Pray to be kept from temptation (Matt. 6:13; Matt. 26:41).
4. Not cause others to be tempted (Rom. 14:13).
5. Restore those overcome by temptation (Gal. 6:1).
6. Avoid temptation (Prov. 4:14-15).

422. WHAT TIME IS IT?

"Behold, now is the accepted time; behold, now is the day of salvation." *II Cor. 6:2*

I. The Time Is Short.
(“Later than you think.” See I Cor. 7:29; Jas. 4:14.)

II. Time to Awake
(Much work to be done. See Rom. 13:12.)

III. Time to Seek the Lord
("While he may be found." See Hos. 10:12.)

IV. Time to Conserve Time
("The night cometh." See Eph. 5:16.)

423. GOD'S PEOPLE

"I will be their God, and they shall be my people."
II Cor. 6:16

God's people are:

1. A chosen people (Deut. 7:6; I Pet. 2:9).
2. A redeemed people. (Exod. 15:13; Eph. 1:7).
3. A peculiar people (Deut. 14:2; Tit. 2:14).
4. A separated people (Exod. 33:16; John 15:19).
5. A holy people (Deut. 7:6; I Pet. 1:15).
6. A happy people (Deut. 33:29; John 15:11).

424. CHRISTIAN GIVING

"Every man according as he purposeth in his heart, so let him give; not grudgingly, or of necessity; for God loveth a cheerful giver." *II Cor. 9:7*

I. Why Give?
1. Because we're stewards, not owners. See Matt. 25:14-30.
2. Because we're commanded to give. See Heb. 13:16.
3. Because of Christ's example. See II Cor. 8:9.
4. For the sake of our example to others. See II Cor. 9:1, 2.
5. For the reflex influence upon ourselves. See Prov. 11:25; Luke 6:38.

II. How Much?
1. As the Lord has prospered us. See I Cor. 16:2.
2. Tithes and offerings. See Mal. 3:10.

425. GOD'S UNSPEAKABLE GIFT

"Thanks be unto God for his unspeakable gift." *II Cor. 9:15*

God's gift is:

1. A precious gift (I Pet. 2:4, 6-7)

2. A promised gift (Gen. 3:15; Isa. 7:14)
3. A perfect gift (Luke 3:22)
4. A priceless gift (Isa. 9:6)
5. A personal gift (John 1:12; 3:16)

—F. W. Phillips

426. TAKING AN INVENTORY

"Examine yourselves, whether ye be in the faith; prove your own selves." *II Cor. 13:5*

Inventory questions:

1. Am I Spirit-led? (Rom. 8:14.)
2. Am I striving to please God in all things? (Ps. 66:18.)
3. Am I cultivating a constant awareness of the presence of God? (Gen. 16:13.)
4. Do I read and love the Scriptures more than any other book? (Ps. 1:2.)
5. Do I live in the spirit of prayer? (Eph. 6:18.)
6. Do I really deny myself for Christ's sake? (Mark 8:34.)
7. Do I relish religious conversation? (Mal. 3:16.)
8. Do I have upon my heart the burden of lost souls? (Jer. 9:1.)
9. Do I remember the Sabbath day and keep it holy? (Exod. 20:8.)
10. Am I living each day in a state of preparation to meet God? (Amos 4:12.)

427. THE CHRISTIAN'S WALK

"Walk worthy of the vocation wherewith ye are called." *Eph. 4:1*

How to walk:

1. Worthily (Eph. 4:1; I Thess. 2:12).
2. Humbly (Mic. 6:8; Eph. 4:17).
3. In love (Eph. 5:2; I John 4:20-21).
4. In the light (Prov. 4:18; John 8:12).
5. With God (Gen. 5:24; I John 1:7).
6. Keep on the King's highway (Isa. 35:8).

428. FIVE ANGRY MEN

"Let not the sun go down upon your wrath." *Eph. 4:26*

At least five Bible characters did themselves and others great harm by losing their tempers and committing rash acts.

I. CAIN
(In a fit of jealous anger he murdered his brother.)

II. MOSES
(Angered by unkind criticism, he struck the rock instead of speaking to it.)

III. BALAAM
(Something irritated him, so he took his vengeance by beating a mule.)

IV. NAAMAN
(Got mad at a preacher—Elisha—because he didn't say the words Naaman wanted to hear.)

V. PETER
(In anger he cut off the ear of the high priest's servant.)

429. GRIEVING THE SPIRIT OF GOD

"Grieve not the holy Spirit of God, whereby ye are sealed unto the day of redemption." *Eph. 4:30*

How men grieve God's Holy Spirit:

1. By tempting him (Acts 5:9).
2. By vexing him (Isa. 63:10).
3. By quenching him (I Thess. 5:19).
4. By lying to him (Acts 5:3-4).
5. By resisting him (Acts 7:51).
6. By undervaluing his gifts (Acts 8:19-20).
7. By trifling with him (Heb. 6:4-6).
8. By disregarding his testimony (Neh. 9:30).
9. By blaspheming against him (Matt. 12:31-32; I John 5:16).

430. BE STRONG!

"Finally, my brethren, be strong in the Lord, and in the power of his might." *Eph. 6:10*

Be strong:

1. In resisting sin (Ps. 119:9; Eph. 6:13)
2. In helping others (Gal. 6:1, 2; Rom. 15:1)
3. In time of trouble (Job 23: 10-12; Ps. 46:1-3)
4. In carrying out Christ's purposes (Mark 16:15; Acts 1:8)

431. POSTURES IN PRAYER

". . . praying always with all prayer and supplication in the Spirit." *Eph. 6:18*

Acceptable prayers have been offered by God's servants in various postures:

1. Standing (I Kings 8:22; Mark 11:25).
2. Bowing down (Ps. 95:6).
3. Kneeling (II Chron. 6:13; Ps. 95:6; Luke 22:41; Acts 20:36).
4. Falling on the face—putting face to the ground (Num. 16:22; Josh. 5:14; I Chron. 21:16; Matt. 26:39).
5. Spreading forth the hands (Isa. 1:15).
6. Lifting up the hands (Ps. 28:2; Lam. 29:19; I Tim. 2:8).

Conclusion: The important thing is to pray in the Spirit. (Eph. 6:18.)

432. BLESSED ASSURANCE

"I know whom I have believed, and am persuaded that he is able to keep that which I have committed unto him against that day." *II Tim. 1:12*

We know:

1. "We have passed from death unto life." (I John 3:14.)
2. We were redeemed by the precious blood of Christ. (I Pet. 1:18-19.)
3. "All things work together for good." (Rom. 8:28.)
4. "We have a building of God, an house not made with hands, eternal in the heavens." (II Cor. 5:1.)
5. Our Redeemer lives, and we shall see him face to face. (Job 19:25-27.)

433. MARCHING TO ZION

"He looked for a city which hath foundations, whose builder and maker is God." *Heb. 11:10*

I. FORGETTING THOSE THINGS WHICH ARE BEHIND (Phil. 3:13)

II. PRESSING FORWARD (Phil. 3:14)

III. SETTING AFFECTIONS ON THINGS ABOVE (Col. 3:2)

IV. VISUALIZING THE UNSEEN HOST, LOOKING THIS WAY (Heb. 12:1)

V. CASTING ASIDE IMPEDIMENTS (Heb. 12:1)

VI. PATIENT PLODDING (Heb. 12:1)

VII. WHAT TO ANTICIPATE (Isa. 35:10)

434. GOOD LOOKS

". . . looking unto Jesus the author and finisher of our faith." *Heb. 12:2*

Look

1. Up (Ps. 5:3; Heb. 12:2).
2. Back (Isa. 51:1).
3. Ahead (II Tim. 4:8).
4. Around (Phil. 2:3-4).
5. Within (II John 8).

435. WRONG USES OF THE TONGUE

"The tongue can no man tame; it is an unruly evil, full of deadly poison." *Jas. 3:8*

Wrong uses of the tongue include:

1. Much talking (Prov. 10:19; 29:11).
2. Idle talking (II Tim. 2:16).

3. Talebearing (Prov. 18:8).
4. Speaking evil of others (Jas. 4:11)
5. False witnessing (Prov. 25:18).
6. Filthy communications (Col. 3:8).
7. Murmuring (I Cor. 10:10).
8. Lying (Ps. 34:13; Col. 3:9).
9. Swearing (Matt. 5:34; Jas. 5:12).

436. PRAYER STATIC

"Ye ask, and receive not, because ye ask amiss, that ye may consume it upon your lusts."
Jas. 4:3

Hindrances to successful prayer:
1. Lack of faith (Jas. 1:6-7).
2. Selfish purposes (Jas. 4:3).
3. An unforgiving spirit (Mark 11:26).
4. Personal pride (Luke 18:11-12).
5. Iniquity in the heart (Ps. 66:18).
6. Refusal to read or hear God's law (Prov. 28:9).
7. Failure to help the poor (Prov. 21:13).

437. TRIED BY FIRE

". . . that the trial of your faith, being much more precious than of gold that perisheth, though it be tried with fire, might be found unto praise and honour and glory at the appearing of Jesus Christ." *I Pet. 1:7*

I. THE METHOD OF TESTING
   1. As silver in the refiner's pot (Prov. 17:3)
   2. As iron in the tempering fire (Isa. 54:16)
II. THE NECESSITY OF TESTING
   1. That we may be obedient (Heb. 11:17)
   2. That we may be pleasing to God (Mal. 3:3-4)
III. THE RESULT OF TESTING
   1. Joy (I Pet. 4:13)
   2. Patience (Jas. 1:3)
IV. THE MEANING OF TESTING
   1. A revelation of God (Job 42:5-6)
   2. A sign of sonship (Heb. 12:6)

—Edith Smith

438. HUMILITY

"Be clothed with humility."
I Pet. 5:5

Humility
1. Is required by God (Mic. 6:8).
2. Was exemplified by Christ (Matt. 11:29; John 13:4-5).
3. Is the beginning of salvation (Job 22:29; Luke 18:13-14).
4. Brings answers to prayer (II Chron. 7:14; Ps. 9:12).
5. Is the secret of revival (Isa. 57:15; 66:2).
6. Is a characteristic of greatness (Prov. 18:12; Matt. 18:4).
7. Is the road to exaltation (Jas. 4:10; I Pet. 5:6).

—N. H. Camp

439. HOW GOD CARES FOR HIS OWN

". . . casting all your care upon him; for he careth for you."
I Pet. 5:7

Symbols of God's care:
1. As a mother comforteth (Isa. 66:13)
2. As a father pitieth (Ps. 103:13)
3. As a nurse cherisheth (I Thess. 2:7)
4. As a shepherd seeketh (Ezek. 34:12)
5. As a hen gathereth (Matt. 23:37)
6. As an eagle fluttereth (Deut. 32:11)
7. As a bridegroom rejoiceth (Isa. 62:5)

—George W. Noble

440. NEW THINGS

"Behold, I make all things new."
Rev. 21:5

1. New birth (John 3:3)
2. New creature (II Cor. 5:17)
3. New song (Ps. 40:3)
4. New life (Col. 3:3)
5. New name (Rev. 2:17)
6. New body (Phil. 3:20-21)
7. New home (John 14:2)

—Elias Christian Goehle

INDEX

(*Numbers in the Index refer to starter numbers.*)